Rethinking the Work Ethic: Embrace the Struggle and Exceed Your Highest Potential

Other Titles By Connie Ragen Green

Doing What It Takes: The Online Entrepreneur's Playbook

Book. Blog. Broadcast. – The Trifecta of Entrepreneurial Success

Write Publish Prosper: How to Write Prolifically, Publish Globally, and Prosper Eternally

The Transformational Entrepreneur: Creating a Life of Dedication and Service

Living the Internet Lifestyle: Quit Your Job, Become an Entrepreneur, and Live Your Ideal Life

The Inner Game of Internet Marketing

The Weekend Marketer: Say Goodbye to the "9 to 5", Build an Online Business, and Live the Life You Love

What is Your Why?

Time Management Strategies for Entrepreneurs: How to Manage Your Time to Increase Your Bottom Line

Huge Profits with Affiliate Marketing: How to Build an Online Empire by Recommending What You Love

Membership Sites Made Simple

Article Marketing: How to Attract New Prospects, Create Products, and Increase Your Income

Targeted Traffic Techniques

Huge Profits With a Tiny List: 50 Ways to Use Relationship Marketing to Increase Your Bottom Line

Rethinking the Work Ethic: Embrace the Struggle and Exceed Your Highest Potential

By
Connie Ragen Green

Copyright © 2017 by Hunter's Moon Publishing

 *ISBN Paperback: 978-1-937988-33-3*
ISBN Kindle: 978-1-937988-34-0

Hunter's Moon Publishing
http://HuntersMoonPublishing.com

Interior Design by Shawn Hansen
Cover Design by Shawn Hansen

Dedication

I have dedicated this book to two people who originally brought the topic of work ethic again into my consciousness and whom continue to inspire me and keep me motivated to embrace the struggle and exceed my highest potential.

The first is Sanna Olkkonen, someone who embodies the strongest work ethic I have ever witnessed. She does so in an unassuming yet powerful way that moves mountains. Her determination and consistency with always carefully thinking through a situation, searching for and finding the logical solution in which everyone will benefit, and then carrying it through to fruition is an example for all of us.

As a result of this way of living, Sanna has been able to accomplish what most of us only dream of - a strong marriage, four amazing children, and a career in the field she was destined to be part of - nursing.

Thank you, Sanna for being a part of my life for all of these years and for embodying the work ethic.

The second is Shawn Hansen, a powerhouse of a human being who helped make the latest reinvention in my business a seamless and joyous process. She has knowledge, skills, and insight into the world of online marketing and entrepreneurship that regularly WOW me.

Shawn has that innate sense of how things can be done in a way that serves everyone and perseveres until the job is complete. Her work ethic precedes her in everything she touches. And her level of integrity to herself, with others, and to the process of life and business is second to none. That is extremely rare in today's world and something I deeply respect and appreciate.

Shawn, without you in my life during these past eighteen months I would have most certainly floundered instead of flourished. Thank you.

Foreword

Being an entrepreneur is a journey - of hard work, excitement, triumphs, disappointments, rewards, and success. Not everyone dreams of being an entrepreneur, but everyone can succeed at it if they have a good model. You've chosen an excellent model in Connie Ragen Green.

When I met Connie nearly a decade ago, three characteristics stood out.

~Enthusiasm
~Willingness to learn
~Persistence

Since then I have watched as Connie applied each of these traits to her ever-expanding online (and offline) business empire.

Her enthusiasm for life, as well as for her business is constantly on display. When you talk to her, you can't help but get excited. Whether she's talking about leading a workshop or writing an article, her "all-in" attitude is contagious.

She loves what she does and she wants you to love what you do as well. She gets excited about an idea - and holds onto it like a terrier with a bone, examining it from every angle, rolling it around, and eventually transforming it into something even better than it started.

Connie never approaches a topic as an "expert." Instead, she maintains a novice's attitude, looking at it with fresh eyes. That's one of the traits that make her such a good coach. She wants to know about your area of expertise, learn all about it, and then help you develop new ways to use that information to your advantage. That transformation in attitude cannot occur if you come at it from an "I am already the expert" perspective. It must emanate from the eyes of an enthusiastic learner.

Most importantly, Connie is persistent. She has faced huge

obstacles in her personal life. Yet she has persisted. She has undergone huge personal and professional transformations and been consistently productive throughout. She never gives up. She may change the path, but she will always arrive at the destination.

Connie didn't start as an entrepreneur. Quite the contrary. She was part of the educational system - a teacher in a Los Angeles city school. And while she loved teaching and helping young children grab the love of learning, she was already preparing for her next move.

Taking classes at night, after a long day in the classroom, Connie earned her real estate license. Those same qualities - enthusiasm, willingness to learn, and persistence - led her to a new career. But she wasn't finished. She was about to embark on her biggest venture yet - Internet Marketing.

Ten years ago there were not a lot of women in the Internet Marketing world, so those of us who were successful in the business were well-known. We did a lot of coaching and people often approached us to do joint ventures with them. While Connie and I had seen each other at a few events, it wasn't until a chance lunch at O'Hare, waiting for our flights that we sat down and talked in depth.

At the conclusion of lunch Connie said "we should do something together" and I agreed. That was Connie's enthusiasm coming through. Of course, I had several people per week say that to me, so I didn't think too much about it.

Less than two weeks later Connie contacted me. "Can we talk about our project," she asked. That was her persistence. So I agreed to a phone call. By the end of that call, we had brainstormed a joint coaching program, set out the timeline for the project, and assigned each task to one or the other of us.

In that first coaching program we quickly learned to work as a team. Connie admitted she didn't know how to do a lot of the things that needed to be done. But she was willing to learn. She was willing to put in the hours and the trial and error it took to get it right. As the program progressed, so did Connie's skills and my respect for her enthusiasm, willingness to learn, and persistence.

That was the first of many coaching programs, information products, and conferences we created and delivered together over the next four years. Connie loved doing all of the personal contacts and answering questions. I took care of all of the technical aspects. She excelled at the marketing, while I loved the logistics. It was a perfect match of skills. And it all began because Connie was enthusiastic, persistent and willing to learn.

One of the most important things you will learn in this book is what I consider Connie's hidden weapon - her consistency. From the beginning, she has used the three traits I've highlighted here to quietly build an empire of content. But even with those, she would still be a run-of-the-mill marketer, if not for her consistency.

When others were writing one article per week for their blogs, Connie was writing one article per day. When others were sending out an email once or twice a week, Connie was sending out an email every day. When others grew tired of coming up with new ideas, Connie continued to crank out the entertaining and engaging content for which she is known. Without her consistent effort, none of those things would be noticed.

You've bought this book because you want to develop your entrepreneurial skills. Heed the lessons in this book as she shares them with you. What appears to be basic is actually quite genius in its simplicity. Remember, it doesn't have to be complex to be effective!

Apply the tasks she outlines in the book, even when they seem mundane. It's the mundane that you can leverage into greatness. Be willing to start small, but be consistent.

Connie has built a loyal following and a very successful business over the past decade - all because of the lessons she shares in this book. You can do the same! If you follow her lead, you can achieve a level of entrepreneurial success that will grant you the lifestyle you want and deserve.

Enjoy the journey! You've chosen a great leader.

Jeanette Cates, PhD
Austin, TX
May, 2017

Preface

This book is about how you, as an individual, can change and transform your life completely with the help of a plan of action in the direction you wish to move. It all begins with the habits that we choose to continue implementing and refining day in and day out until they define us. Just as Aristotle stated so succinctly, "we are what we repeatedly do".

Work ethic is the vehicle with which to arrive more quickly at your destination with these repeated habits. The research in the area of work ethic and life transformation is abundant, and that is the area I hope you are interested in learning more about from the experiences and examples I am sharing. I will teach you how to change your thoughts, actions, and beliefs on the way to changing your behavior and nature through daily habits and the rethinking of your work ethic. With these tools, anything is possible in your life.

I am not a sociologist, psychologist, historian, economist, theologian, or someone who has invested in a lifetime of research and study in the areas of social science and humanities that are discussed within these pages. Instead, I am an entrepreneur in the process of becoming the person I am meant to be through these same principles as I am teaching you. Every day, one step at a time, and one change at a time makes this work a worthwhile endeavor.

It is my sincerest hope that this describes you - someone who is open to learning from the experiences of others as a platform from which to catapult yourself to success. This book has been written for those whom are also interested in knowing more and living a life of overcoming challenges and obstacles, embracing life's ongoing struggles, seeking enlightenment, and basking in spiritual and intellectual growth as they pursue entrepreneurship and excellence in how they live their lives and serve others. It is my intention within these pages to discuss and share the thoughts, ideas, and concepts that have moved me along in my journey and continue to be a direct reflection of my life.

This book is more than one you read; it's one you "do". By that I mean that I want you to keep a journal or notebook while you are reading to be able to quickly write down what comes up for you as I introduce you to the thoughts, ideas, and concepts that arise from this topic of rethinking the work ethic. There are also questions and action steps at the end of each section to think about, answer, and write down that will help to make your process go more smoothly and in the direction that will best serve your goals and aspirations.

I want you to dig deep to think about and remember how you were first introduced to the concept of a work ethic. Did it come from your parents or other family members, or a coach, a teacher, or a book you read in high school? Or was it much later, perhaps when you were at your first job or in graduate school? What if the way you perceive your own work ethic could predict and determine your future successes in life and in business?

This book is intended to get you on the right track, or perhaps a new track as a human being, as well as an entrepreneur. And if it's hard work that will get us closer to where we want to be, I am ready for that and hope that you are on board as well. We can all compete on a level playing field and accomplish goals beyond our wildest dreams if hard work and a strong work ethic are the determining factors.

Connie Ragen Green
May, 2017

Table of Contents

Introduction

A person who wants to lead the orchestra
must turn their back on the crowd.
~ Max Lucado

When I began to formulate the idea for this book within the depths of my mind during the spring of 2016, I honestly wasn't sure where to begin. It seemed that overnight I had once again begun hearing discussions around and reading articles about the work ethic and how it had been eroding over the years. In choosing this as the topic for this book (my fifteenth), I pledged to investigate, explore, and discover just what was meant by these statements. I had so many questions that caused me to reevaluate my own values, beliefs, and behavior around this substantially important topic. Was the work ethic eroding to the point of no return? Whose responsibility would it be to rethink it and bring this to the forefront of our vision and focus for future generations? How could I best serve others by getting involved in this discussion?

Even if the media was using this as a way to get our attention and the conversation started, it seemed worthwhile for me to acknowledge that and to share my own thoughts and ideas on work ethic, in relation to entrepreneurship and achieving at least a modicum of success in life and in business. Every idea has to start somewhere, and I could think of no better place for a humble beginning than within the broadcast and narrow cast venues of this new millennium, as it unfolded on the internet and beyond.

During my twenty years as a classroom teacher I could remember more than one administrator bragging about the teachers who "worked hard". I was never included in this group, or at least my perception during that time was that I was being excluded, and I questioned what this meant to me. I came to the conclusion that I had never taken it upon myself to work hard. Instead, I valued the concepts of working smart, and of balancing work with more joyful activities away from work, and of leaving the hard work to the blue collar workers instead of the professionals.

Clearly, I was missing something in the bigger picture but had no idea of what it could be at that time in my life. In retrospect I know that my work ethic was by no means a focus or a concern in my efforts to live a productive life and that was obvious with every step I took and in the results I achieved.

In the first section of this book I discuss the origin and the meaning of this key phrase and how it is currently interpreted by people across the globe. We explore what is meant by "the struggle" and why you must embrace this if you are to grow and have the ability to move to the next level personally and in your business.

This is followed by a discussion of just why the concept of having a work ethic is so crucial to success on any level. Many of us settled for a life of mediocrity and slogged away at a job that we did not love for many years. That's when some of us decided that perhaps Eleanor Roosevelt was correct in saying that we must "do that thing we cannot do". It certainly continues to ring true for me and for others to this very day. Many people have reached heights they never thought possible by changing their perspective on the work ethic and I will share some of their stories with you.

Next, we explore the possibilities of just what is possible once you embrace a work ethic in your own life. Seeing your life and your business in a new light will change everything you say, do, and have in the future. It's the difference between approaching life and business as relational instead of simply transactional. This concept alone will change your life.

Finally, I share exactly how you can rethink your own work ethic and increase your productivity and results. This is where we roll up our sleeves and dig in to what needs to happen with your thinking, actions, and beliefs so that you can change your nature as a result of this work.

Rethinking the Work Ethic: Embrace the Struggle and Exceed Your Highest Potential explores why some people are more successful than others based on what they do every single day. Is it the discipline and determination to do a good job and finish what you start, or is it something much deeper ingrained in the mind of the accomplished person? You will come to your own conclusions on these and many other questions, but know that you must turn your back on the crowd if you truly want to lead the orchestra with your music.

Part I
What Is a Work Ethic?

More than likely you first came across the phrase "work ethic" at some point in your younger life. It may have been from your parents or other family members, or from teachers or other significant, influential adults in your life. Or perhaps it was from someone you worked for at an early job or at the beginning of your career. Depending upon the circumstances under which you were first exposed to this concept you came to your own conclusions as to its meaning, value, and application to your own life and you may not have evaluated your initial impression since it was first implanted and accepted in your mind.

The intention of this first section is to first define what this concept of "work ethic" has come to mean over the past few centuries, to discuss what it means to "embrace the struggle", and to then explore the work ethic in terms of how you have come to live your life on a daily basis. We'll look at why making ever so slight, yet noticeable changes to your thinking, behavior, and actions will allow you to change your nature. That is when you will be able to achieve more than you ever thought possible and to exceed your highest potential. Finally, I'll share which actions will best serve you as you move your thinking and behavior forward.

Remember that anyone can achieve what I am presenting here, and that it takes hard work and determination to make that happen consistently. Get into the habit of daily practice at whatever you wish to excel in and your proficiency will grow exponentially over time.

At the end of this and of all of the sections I will include activities and additional questions that will guide you to the conclusions you will be able to base your actions on during the next phase of your life. I eagerly await this opportunity to serve you. Let's begin your journey...

Defining Work Ethic

Determine never to be idle... It is wonderful
how much may be done if we are always doing.
~ Thomas Jefferson

I will now define the term work ethic to mean the principle that hard work is intrinsically virtuous or worthy of reward. This is a value based on simultaneous hard work and diligence. And a work ethic is not just comprised of hard work but also of a set of accompanying virtues.

The above paragraph will be the basis of our discovery and exploration of this concept as we make our way through these pages.

When I ask you to "rethink the work ethic" what I mean is that many of us lack the very skills and behaviors associated with the concept of work ethic and are living and experiencing our lives in a way that proves how important this is to our overall success and well-being. Even if you were raised with or developed your own work ethic along the way there is room for improvement and change in how what you are currently doing serves you day by day. By rethinking what we are actually *doing* each day we have the opportunity to bring about meaningful change to everything in our lives.

I now want you to dig deep to think about and remember how you were first introduced to the concept of a work ethic. Previously I stated that this was most likely a parent or other adult family member, from a teacher or clergyman, or from a boss or supervisor.

But you may have a very different memory of your introduction to this topic, as was the case in my life experience, which you may be able to relate to in your own life.

I was in my senior year at UCLA when I was first aware of a

discussion around the topic of work ethic. It was in a class on comparative English literature, economics, and sociology where this phrase was first introduced. I needed both the units and the subject matter to graduate that spring with a dual major of political science and psychobiology and had no idea what to expect.

What was to come over the following three and a half months made my head spin. My thinking, actions, and beliefs were in for an awakening, one that I would not fully take to heart and put into practice until three decades later.

It turned out that I had not been raised with a work ethic at all, and that everything I engaged in was left mostly to chance or to luck. Of course my first twenty years of life had been a struggle; I had no compass to give me direction. Let's go back in time before we return to the present day in regards to exploring the work ethic as a concept.

Political Ideas on Work Ethic

If we want to explore a politically based definition of work ethic, these definitions are presented in a historical context:

Socialists believe that the concept of "hard work" is meant to delude the working class into being loyal servants to the elite, and that working hard, in itself, is not automatically an honorable thing, but only a means to creating more wealth for the people at the top of the economic pyramid.

Marxists think "work ethic" is not a useful sociological concept. They argue having a "work ethic" in excess of management's control doesn't appear rational in any mature industry where the employee can't rationally hope to become more than a manager whose fate still depends on the owner's decisions. They view the cultural ingrainment of this value as a means to delude the working class into creating more wealth for the upper class. The French Leftist philosopher André Gorz wrote:

"The work ethic has now become obsolete. It is no longer true that producing more means working more, or that producing more will lead to a better way of life.

The connection between more and better has been broken; our needs for many products and services are already more than adequately met, and many of our as-yet- unsatisfied needs will be met not by producing more, but by producing differently, producing other things, or even producing less. This is especially true as regards our needs for air, water, space, silence, beauty, time and human contact.

Neither is it true any longer that the more each individual works, the better off everyone will be. In a post-industrial society, not everyone has to work hard in order to survive, though may be forced to anyway due to the economic system. The present crisis has stimulated technological change of an unprecedented scale and speed: 'the micro-chip revolution'. The object and indeed the effect of this revolution has been to make rapidly increasing savings in labour, in the industrial, administrative and service sectors. Increasing production is secured in these sectors by decreasing amounts of labour. As a result, the social process of production no longer needs everyone to work in it on a full-time basis. The work ethic ceases to be viable in such a situation and workbased society is thrown into crisis."

And the Capitalist view is that a work ethic refers not just to hard work but also to a set of accompanying virtues, whose crucial role is in the development and sustaining of free markets globally. Benjamin Franklin wrote this:

"Remember, that time is money. He that can earn ten shillings a day by his labor, and goes abroad, or sits idle, one half of that day, though he spends but sixpence during his diversion or idleness, ought not to reckon that the only expense; he has really spent, or rather thrown away, five shillings besides. Remember, that money is the prolific, generating nature. Money can beget money, and its offspring can beget more, and so on. Five shillings turned is six, turned again is seven and threepence, and so on, till it becomes a hundred pounds. The more there is of it, the more it produces every turning, so that the profits rise quicker and quicker. He that kills a breeding sow, destroys all her offspring to the thousandth generation. He that murders a crown, destroys all that it might have produced, even scores of pounds."

This is a statement filled with moral language and ideas. It is in effect an ethical response to the natural desire for hedonic reward, a statement of the value of delayed gratification to achieve self-actualization. Indeed, Benjamin Franklin claims that God revealed to him the usefulness of virtue.

Let's now move on to religion as the basis of work ethic.

Religious Thinking on Work Ethic

Here are some religious beliefs on this topic that you may be familiar with. Remember that these are generalized for the purpose of this discussion and that you may have heard different versions throughout your childhood and beyond.

The Protestant work ethic, the Calvinist work ethic or the Puritan work ethic is a concept in theology, sociology, economics and history which emphasizes that hard work, discipline and frugality are a result of a person's salvation in the Protestant faith. This is in contrast to Roman Catholic tradition which emphasizes religious attendance, confession and ceremonial sacrament. A person does not need to be religious in order to follow or be affected by the Protestant work ethic, as it is ingrained in certain cultures and has become a part of the DNA.

My memories do not include being indoctrinated with any of these ideas throughout my somewhat limited religious upbringing.

What about a person's gender or ethnicity or other status? Does work ethic have anything to do with how much income our parents earned or in which part of the world we grew up?

Work Ethic Related to Age, Gender, Ethnicity, Socio-Economic Status, or Geographical Location

Having been born in and currently living in the state of California for most of my life I know that we have the reputation of not doing what we say we will do and of not following through in general. I first heard this belief from some of the people I was attending law school with in New York back in the late 1970s and was shocked to know they had made this type of generalization of Californians. But over the following years I came to understand what they were referring to with this blanket statement.

Even I was living up to the stereotype of being someone who preferred an easier life than my Southern, Midwestern, Pacific Northwestern, Eastern, or New England counterparts were willing to endure. Yes, I expected the sun to shine each day and yes, I believed it was my right to be able to drive each day instead of taking public transportation. And I dressed the part as well, preferring jeans and colorful shirts to dressier, more business-like attire.

But along with my attitudes and clothing came the mindset of someone who was not willing to do what it takes to be successful. Back then I looked for an easier way out of situations and also made excuses that gave me reasons instead of results.

But was it really that simple? Did people have less of a work ethic based on their age, gender, socio-economic status, or geographical location? Again, I am not a social scientist but I believe very strongly in my informal research and findings.

People all over our planet have more similarities than differences. And no matter what labels we all use to describe others there is a common thread that runs through each of us. It is the desire to thrive and succeed in the areas that hold importance for us at any specific point in time. These include, but are not limited to our desire to do our best when it comes to relationships, earning a living, helping others, and achieving our dreams and goals. More specifically these areas of life could include parenting, running a business, building a home, overcoming a physical or mental challenge, pursuing a career, and making a name for ourselves in a variety of areas in our life.

What I Believe to Be the Truth

My definition of the work ethic stems from my experiences, beliefs, observations, and values over my lifetime, as would be expected.

I was raised as an only child in a single parent home, and my mother did her best to instill the notion of right and wrong in me from a young ago. We were in poverty until I was about twelve years old, at which time I began to work and contribute some money to our household through babysitting, mowing lawns, scraping barnacles from the bottoms of wooden boats, dog walking, and other odd jobs around the neighborhood.

This additional income made it much easier for us to go about our day to day life without worrying where our next meal would come from or if we would be evicted from our apartment. But it did absolutely nothing to alleviate our fears of what the next day might bring. I believe this was due to my mother continually slipping back into old habits, beliefs, and actions that did not serve us.

A strong work ethic, or for that matter a work ethic of any kind did not make its way into the equation. Instead, I was raised to always "try your best" when it came to academics, sports, and all aspects of my young life. This is like trying to play darts while blindfolded or being told to run the fastest in the race when you can't see the other runners.

If I wanted to try something my mother was supportive. If I decided to quit, she was supportive of that as well. The only time I can remember her pleading with me not to give up on something was when she was teaching me how to play the piano. She had played from a young age and our church gave permission for us to use their piano several times a week.

I can still remember the shiny silver key the preacher had made for us. We kept it on a leather shoelace so it wouldn't get lost. Running ahead to unlock the side door of the church, I would look back at my mother making her way up the grassy hill, her arms filled with music books and notebooks and then meet her halfway to ease her load.

But I was a whiny and impatient child and as a twelve-year-old did not enjoy practicing my scales and the simple songs she was teaching me for endless hours. So when it went on for several weeks in a row I complained that if I couldn't learn to play more difficult and popular tunes I just wanted to quit piano altogether.

My mother made her strongest case for me to continue learning and practicing. She made some excellent points about what it meant to be able to play the piano. It could lead to other things, like singing. After I learned some classical pieces I could switch to popular music. She extolled the virtues of being a musician and of being able to sit down at the piano and play music for others as I grew older. But in the end she caved to my strong will and it was never mentioned again. To this day I regret not sticking with it and following her requests that I continue.

After that time my mother and I returned to a life of each of us trying our best and neither of us accomplishing much. It was the path of least resistance, filled with mediocrity, and one that leads quickly to unremarkable results and lackluster complacency. But at least we tried - sigh.

The Struggle

Where there is no struggle, there is no strength.
~ Oprah Winfrey

Please remember as you are reading here that I am discussing the work ethic in regards to entrepreneurship. Even though I introduced the concept in the previous chapter by sharing the historically accepted political and religious beliefs around this topic, the true value of what I am sharing with you here is in how you will view your current life, mission, and vision throughout the remainder of your life by shaping and developing a work ethic that will serve you and those around you. Ultimately it is you who will determine how you choose to spend every moment of every day.

When I ask you to "rethink the work ethic" what I really intend for you to do is to realize and accept that anything worth achieving in life will be a struggle. Those who choose not to tackle this struggle head on risk not achieving their goals at a level that challenges them to reach, and even exceed their highest potential. Those who welcome the struggle are destined to prosper and live lives filled with joy and even miraculous results. Know that if any of this was easy, then everyone would achieve great success.

The choice is yours. Choose wisely.

Been There, Done That

You may be thinking that you've already experienced one or more struggles in your life related to jobs, careers, investments, health challenges, relationships, or in other areas. This may be the basis for your belief that after you have already "been there and done that" you deserve to have more success without going through another struggle.

This is not possible because you are attempting to reach a new level in your life and thinking, and you will simply plateau if you try to get to this new level by doing what you have done in the past. It will not work and your level of frustration will increase as you continue to bang your head against the wall.

Instead, embrace this struggle and view it as the opportunity to reach higher and ask for more than you have ever done before. There are so many analogies I could draw here to make my point, and I have chosen one from my own life experience to demonstrate how this can work in your favor.

When I decided to become a classroom teacher I had no idea what to expect. The year was 1986 and the Space Shuttle Challenger tragedy with high school teacher Christa McAuliffe aboard had just occurred. Within eight months I had made the decision to return to school, applied for and received an Emergency Credential to teach in the inner city of Los Angeles public schools, and had been assigned to a combination fifth and sixth grade self-contained classroom.

Over the next eighteen years I honed my skills, attended additional classes and programs on a variety of topics, and learned about technology on my own. Some years I was more creative and innovative than in others, receiving two technology grants for my classroom and some other accolades for my teaching style and results. But most years I just maintained the status quo. During those years I did what the majority of the other teachers at my school site were doing. It seemed like I wasn't even curious about what was possible because I was so busy doing only what was expected of me and nothing more.

Then one summer a teacher transferred to my school from a neighboring one. He had experienced challenges at that school and finally applied for this transfer. The gossip flew as teachers speculated about what the reason could have been. On the first day of classroom setup before the students arrived I was the only one to visit his classroom and welcome him to our school.

Mark and I became fast friends and within a couple of days it was obvious to me that he did things very differently than I had become accustomed to doing during my teaching career. He was setting up his classroom in such a way that it seemed like it was for high school students instead of elementary age children. There were posters and bulletin boards and specialized areas we refer to as "centers" that challenged the students' cognitive thinking skills and introduced concepts far advanced from anything I had ever seen in a classroom setting. I wanted to be in Mark's class! For each of the following two days I visited his room and watched him prepare and add to the learning adventure that was unfolding before my very eyes.

By the third day I couldn't stand it any longer and I asked him about his work as a classroom teacher. This turned into an hours long discussion of everything from what he had learned as a part of a "master teacher" program to what his expectations were of the children who would pass through his door each year.

I remember going home that Friday night and having mixed feelings about what Mark and I had discussed and the concepts and perspectives he had shared with me. Was it possible that I was not teaching to the same standards as other teachers? Had I become complacent over the years? Did I even know how to be the best teacher I could be?

All weekend long I sat with these questions and feelings and by the time Monday morning rolled around I was a changed person. Or at least I had changed my thinking dramatically and was on my way to becoming a changed person, at least when it came to my teaching.

What had changed was my commitment to achieving, maintaining, and surpassing my work ethic. Even though I had been in the classroom, or in the "trenches" as many teachers described it for those eighteen years, I was now on my way to reaching a new paradigm in my work. I was willing to embrace the struggle that was sure to be ahead of me so that I could reach and then exceed my own potential.

Next I needed to change not only my thinking, but also my actions, beliefs, and behaviors. This is necessary so that you can in turn change your nature. I'll discuss this further later on in this book. I was in for the ride of my life, and this journey was the beginning of my being able to change my life completely and dramatically.

As a result of this new friendship, as well as a number of other things that coincidentally occurred in my life that year, the next two years would be my final ones as a classroom teacher. It was wonderful to have my life transformation at this time so that I could finally be the teacher I intended to be and to leave this profession on a high note.

Recently I looked up Mark to see what he was doing these days. Soon after I left teaching he was inspired to leave the public school system and teach in the private sector, where he continues to share his wisdom and vision with the children and adults who are fortunate enough to be a part of his world.

If you have ever found yourself thinking, feeling, or saying out loud that you have already "been there and done that" and do not wish to go through those experiences again, know that you are resisting the struggle that will be required to take you to the next level in your life or business that you are yearning for. Instead of dreading the thoughts, actions, and behaviors that will take you there, it is my strong recommendation that you move forward logically and enthusiastically.

Making It Happen

*Researchers have settled on what they believe is the magic
number for true expertise: ten thousand hours.*
~ Malcolm Gladwell

It is said that talk is cheap and that you must be willing to take action on your beliefs and values if they are to ever come to fruition. That was my dilemma as I set about rethinking my work ethic as a classroom teacher. I'll come back to my story after we explore more on this topic of making things happen in your life.

Let's begin with a discussion on the hard work required to level up your work ethic. But first, what values does a hard worker possess? A hard worker is someone who stays on task without needing close supervision to do so; a person who puts forth consistent, good effort without taking excessive or unnecessary breaks, and an individual who continues to work hard even when tired, preoccupied, or not supervised. So, the type of hard work I am referring to requires independence, consistency, and perseverance. These are also the values and actions of those pursuing their highest potential at all times.

Few of us reach anything close to our full potential during our lifetimes, let along reaching for our highest potential. Instead we go about our life and work each day, satisfied to live a life of mediocrity. It's sad but true and I will now share why I honestly believe this to be the case.

Life isn't easy. It also isn't fair. Add to this the overwhelming demands on our time and thought processes just to make ends meet and do everything we need to do for ourselves and our loved ones. It is a wonder anyone ever goes above and beyond what is required of them to achieve something special. But many people on our planet who have much less innate intelligence, resources, privileges, and connections than you and I already possess do so every single day of their life, and many do it on a regular basis.

So why can't you be one of them? The short answer is that you can, if you choose this path.

Your Ten Thousand Hours

Malcolm Gladwell's quote at the beginning of this chapter is an important concept to review and ponder. For now I want you to start thinking about everything you do in terms of this "ten thousand hours" rule. For everything you decide to take on in your life, ask yourself if you are willing to put in your ten thousand hours, or anything even close to that amount of time.

The idea of the ten thousand hours is based upon the widely accepted belief that it will take this long to master a skill. This rule has been applied to sports, music, academia, and more. As a classroom teacher I was able to put in my ten thousand hours within the first three years or so because of my enthusiasm and willingness to learn and implement what I was learning. When I decided to become a writer in 2006 I made the conscious decision to put in my ten thousand hours as quickly as possible to take me to the next level with my skill. But most of us are not consistent with this. Here's an example.

Two years ago I once again decided I wanted to learn how to play the ukulele. The first question I (again) asked myself was if I was willing to put in the required ten thousand hours to master this skill. I thought I was, but my actions and behavior over this time period have proved otherwise. As a result, I still can't even play one song all the way through without following my notes, and each time I pick up my instrument I fumble while tuning it and getting my fingers in the correct place to play. I'm sure I will revisit this at some point in the future, but for now I am okay with knowing that it is my choice to not put in the time.

Know that you alone are in charge of what you choose to achieve. You may change your mind at any time, go back to something you previously wanted to achieve, and completely rework your original thoughts and ideas. It's always up to you and only you to choose your path. Let your work ethic and your conscience be your guide.

When it comes to making it happen I am reminded of people living in remote areas of our world who struggle to provide clean drinking water for their families every day. You and I cannot possibly imagine what it is like to wake up each morning and worry about where we will find clean water for drinking, cooking, and bathing that day. So when you think about the hardships of your present situation, where most of what we deal with it a far cry from being a life or death matter think about those who are truly in need each day of their lives. These people must develop a strong work ethic and be willing to work hard each day in order to just stay alive.

Going back to my teaching days I have a vivid memory of one of the administrators admonishing teachers regularly for not working hard. At some point I came to the realization that it had not ever been my goal to work hard. I wanted instead to work smart, to be able to take shortcuts, and to get to the point where everything would come to me more easily. But that became an uphill battle and I was filled with resistance. At that time I wasn't willing to do the work, and to do it joyfully.

It was eighteen years into my career as a classroom teacher when I finally understood the value of working hard on a consistent basis in all areas of my life. This was in part due to the inspiration, motivation, and guidance I received from the fellow teacher I told you about earlier.

Once I had achieved my basis of ten thousands hours of teaching, which occurred at some point during my third year in the classroom I needed to then focus my time and attention on exceeding my highest potential. This correlates to tactics and strategies in the business world. Instead, I stayed where I was and resisted the change that had to begin and end with me and my actions and behaviors so that I could change my nature and become the teacher I would finally become so many years later.

Making It Happen for Entrepreneurs

I have written this book primarily for entrepreneurs who are looking for an edge, a distinct and a possibly unfair advantage in their businesses to help them to achieve success over and above anything they previously thought was possible. Lean in closer, for this is where I share the first secret of exactly how to do this...

...work hard each minute of every day!

Yes, that's all it takes to begin this process of making it happen and exceeding your highest potential. Now I will go on to explain how to change yourself from the inside out so that you become a high performer each day without giving it a second thought. And I will promise you that once you become accustomed to working at a higher level each day you will not have any desire to go back to where you were before. In fact, you may find it impossible to work at a slower pace or to be willing to spend the time and energy to achieve so little. You will be on fire and feel like you have super powers!

I like to think about this as a life and death situation where "survival of the fittest" comes into play. Remember earlier when I mentioned that people all over our planet are engaged in finding and transporting clean water back to their villages each day? You know that they must work hard each day in order to achieve this goal because their continued existence and life is at stake. Fortunately we are not in the same situation, but the way I see it is that we must act as though our lives depend on it just as the villagers do if we are to truly change our natures.

At the beginning of this chapter I offered a quote by author Malcolm Gladwell taken from his 2008 international bestseller *Outliers*. This is now known as the "ten thousand hour rule" and states that it takes roughly ten thousand hours of practice to achieve mastery in a field.

Now this isn't ten thousand hours of thinking about your topic, or telling someone else about it, or making some notes about it. Instead, this requires ten thousand hours of actually doing the work. Focused work. Meaningful work. Hard work. Work!

I have been working with new entrepreneurs in the online space for nearly a decade now. When they come to me they have hundreds of ideas about what they want to achieve in their businesses. If I continue to work with them over the next year or so my intention is to get them to focus on just a few of those early goals to see them through to fruition. Then the resistance comes when they discover that entrepreneurship is quite similar to any small business you might start or a career or even a job in that it all must be broken down into smaller chunks that can be accomplished one at a time.

For example, many entrepreneurs would like to write a book. This might be you right now. You are already sold on the idea that authorship is a worthwhile endeavor. You may even have some ideas about what your book would be about. Perhaps you already have a catchy title that you've shared with family members and close friends who agree that you must write a book.

Then you choose a time to write for an hour. You turn on your computer, open your word processing program, and stare at the blank page. But you won't allow this to be daunting or scary. You have a story to tell and you begin to type it out. Twenty minutes later you are drained from pouring out your heart and mind on the page. You go back and add a few more details and think of one or two more things you want to include.

And then it happens. You are out of ideas and can't imagine what else to write. You are intellectually spent for that day.

The next day you begin looking for the "easy button" for writing a book. You find books on how to do it quickly and easily. Then you find eBooks that promise to help you write a book in seven days. Information products abound which are filled with ideas on how to write more quickly, choose a keyword rich title, achieve bestseller status, turn your book into an online course, and so much more. And there is even software to help you use content from other sources to put together into a book. I will tell you that all of what I have mentioned does exist, and I continue to sell my own courses on how I write my books within a four to six week period and then repurpose them into online courses. But I will tell you that nothing will take the place of you making it happen with hard work, focus, and attention to your project.

This is the work ethic in action, and once you adopt one for yourself your life will be easier. It will also be more rewarding, more lucrative, and increasingly more interesting.

In my example of writing a book I had to rethink my own work ethic to change and simplify my process. This book you are reading now is my fifteenth, and once again it was completed in less than six weeks, this time during the spring of 2017. My secret? Lean in close once again and I will whisper it to you...

I begin with a couple of pages of notes around the topic I will be writing about, from those notes I create an outline, and it is only then that I start the actual writing process. Somewhere around ten thousand words it becomes like filling in the blanks for each chapter. This process feels like I am simply a conduit for the thoughts, ideas, and words that are flowing through me. I had heard about this writing process years ago from other authors and did not realize that by simply applying my newly formed work ethic to any project I wish to complete it would all come together in a timely manner and in a way that felt right to me in regards to my goals. You and everyone else can achieve this or a similar goal when it comes to writing and authorship.

Yes, I have put in my ten thousand hours as a writer by writing blog posts, short reports, eBooks, articles, presentations, emails to my community, and more. My first book, *Huge Profits with a Tiny List - 50 Ways to Use Relationship Marketing to Increase Your Bottom Line* was actually a compilation of fifty blog posts and articles that I repurposed into a full length book. It went on to become a bestseller in 2010 and launched my career as an online marketing strategist, trainer, mentor, and bestselling author.

Be willing to put in the dedicated hours and your goals and dreams will become your reality.

Do This...Don't Do That!

Perfection is not attainable, but if we
chase perfection we can catch excellence.
~ Vince Lombardi

In this first section I have shared the historical meaning of the phrase work ethic, why embracing the struggle will have such profound consequences in your life's journey, and the significance of taking action and making the things you want as a part of your life experience to actually occur and manifest in untold ways.

Now it's time to think about not only what to do, but also what *not* to do. In other words, this chapter is about what I mean when I am asking you to rethink your work ethic to change your life.

None of this is about perfection. Run from that imperfect concept as fast as you can and never, ever look back! The ideology of perfection has brought pain, unhappiness, and a lack of confidence to many throughout the ages. The pursuit of excellence builds self-esteem and moves you closer to success. Make a sign to post near your computer that says "Excellence, not perfection" and read it aloud every day when you sit down to begin your work. And I like the above quote on this subject from Vince Lombardi.

These are the things I do not want you to do as you go through this book and learn more about how thinking about and adjusting your work ethic can help you to change your life:

- Do not allow others to dictate the path you will travel throughout your lifetime. This includes parents, teachers, friends, spouses, children, and employers. No one else can ever know what it is like to walk in your shoes.
- Do not spend time with people who think small, or make you feel small in any way. If you find yourself surrounded by

these people, be polite and make an excuse to escape as quickly as possible. If you live or work with this type of person, make it your goal to learn how to remain focused and positive and to not lose yourself while in their presence.

- Do not believe that you don't have the time or the money to do the things you truly want to do in your life. For more than twenty years I told myself a story that I would spend time volunteering and donate money to charities once I had more time and more money. Once I left my previous life as a classroom teacher and real estate broker/appraiser behind I saw that I had always had some extra time and money to do this. Even though it might have only been three or four hours a month and less than fifty dollars a month I could have made a difference in other people's lives much sooner.
- Don't get caught up with comparing yourself to others or in feeling like there is not enough for you to have what you want. That is a "lack" mentality that you must abandon. An infant does not compare itself to other infants when he or she knows it is time to pull themselves up and take that first step. Instead, they keep trying and eventually stand and walk upright for the remainder of their life.
- Do not allow negative thoughts to take over your thinking. Banish those thoughts with positive affirmations. When you find yourself moving into this space, take time to reflect on all you have to be thankful and grateful for in your life.

Now that I have shared what I do not want you to do, here is the good news about what we must all do. Instead of engaging in thoughts and actions that will not serve you, do these things regularly:
- Trust your instincts, feelings, and intuition as to what is right for you as an individual and then go after your dreams and goals. You know down deep inside of yourself what makes your heart sing, so reach down and pull it out for the rest of the world to see and enjoy.
- Choose friends and business associates who believe in you and your ideas. I have a friend who thinks bigger than almost anyone I know. One day she said to me that her life was too small for her and she set about enlarging her vision and

going even bigger. That thinking and action will change not only her life, but also the lives of many people in the world. We can all do this effectively by surrounding ourselves with the right people. I first found these people in my local Rotary Club, where I became a member when first leaving my previous life behind and coming online in 2006. Now I find these people most everywhere I am because I am focused on finding them.

- Understand and believe that there will always be enough of anything you want to go around. This is "abundance" thinking. When I drive into the parking area of a crowded shopping center I can always find a space right up front. Even though I prefer to park further away to get more exercise I continue to test out this concept each time I'm at a shopping center and have never been disappointed. And driving right on past this prime spot and allowing the person behind me to take it brings me great joy.

- Believe that you can achieve anything at any age, no matter what your background, education, or work experience has been. Previous behavior and results will never be an indicator of future success. For some reason we all get into this type of thinking, but I will challenge you to shift your thinking and give yourself and others the credit they deserve, in advance of achieving it. Treat others as if they have already achieved their goals and dreams and are accomplished in their chosen field.

- Know that you are always in the process of becoming the person you want to be, and that you will never run out of goals and dreams you wish to experience in this lifetime. While I was a classroom teacher I regularly worked with children who believed they were already their final product. Once I taught them this concept of all of us, including myself, being in *the process of becoming* their attitudes, actions, and behavior shifted significantly. It can be quite freeing to know and understand that we can do, have, and become anyone and anything we desire.

I hope these concepts and ideas will be helpful to you and that you will consider making them a part of your new life as a high performer who continues to exceed your own potential.

Part I Action Steps

There is no fatigue so wearisome as that which comes from lack of work.
~ Charles Spurgeon

I introduced the Preface to this book with a quote from Aristotle that goes like this:

We do not act rightly because we have virtue.
We are what we repeatedly do.
Excellence, then, is not an act but a habit.

So let's begin with the habits that you already possess. More than likely you have learned both by being taught and guided by others, as well as by trial and error which habits serve your goals and desires.

Make a list of the habits you deem to be of importance in your life today. Whether they be mundane, such as brushing and flossing each morning and night, or revolutionary, such as running five miles each day before breakfast list them in your journal and notebook.

Now for each habit, add something to it that explains why it is important to you. Here is an example of my intention with this:

I write five hundred to a thousand words each morning, at least five mornings a week because this helps me to achieve my goals of writing blog posts, short reports and full length books.

Here's another example:

I reach out to at least one person in my online business every single day so they will know that I care about and appreciate them. Working as an online entrepreneur is solitary and this exercise provides a social and business connection that enriches each of our lives. It's also extremely good for each person's business.

Now write down some of your habits and why they are important to you. In sales copy this would be referred to as "features and benefits", where the features are what it is and the benefits are what it does for you.

Rethinking Your Work Ethic

Now let's go back to the beginning, where we took a look at the term "work ethic" and I began to unfold my ideas on what it has meant historically, both politically and in religious terms. What does this term mean to you, and what will it mean for you to "rethink" your work ethic as you work your way through this book?

Your Ten Thousand Hours

Where have you put in your ten thousand hours during your life? Many of us have put in this time with driving a car, learning to play a musical instrument, or participating in a sport or other activity. You also may have reached this level at a job or in a career.

When it comes to business skills, which according to Brian Tracy are all "learnable" skills, which ones have you focused on already? Which ones will you focus on in the near future? Writing, teaching online, public speaking, and mentoring are the skills that make the most sense for me to put more hours of practice into. How about you?

Embracing the Struggle

How do think about life and business in terms of struggle? Do you welcome the challenge of learning and taking on something new? Or do you groan and wish that you did not have to do this?

Write down the struggles you anticipate encountering as you move forward. Include as many details as possible, even though it may be slightly painful to do so. Listing the steps in any new venture makes you more aware of the work that will need to be done before you can achieve even a modicum of success.

As you think about and write these down, use the same strategy I introduced you to with your habits, which is to write them with both the features and the benefits.

In my case, I knew that writing and technology would be struggles for me as a new online entrepreneur. I decided to embrace these by writing each day so that my skills would improve and become a habit and to learn just the areas of technology that I needed at my fingertips and to outsource the remainder of them to people who were already skilled and enjoyed doing this work for others.

Author's Note: It is my wish that you do not proceed to the next section in this book until you have spent some time thinking about and then writing down your thoughts on the above mentioned items. It is in this way that you will be able to fully comprehend and implement my teaching on these topics so that you can more fully benefit from these ideas and concepts.

Part II
Why Is Work Ethic So Crucial?

I've never viewed myself as particularly talented. Where I excel is ridiculous, sickening work ethic. While the other guy is sleeping, I'm working. While he's eating, I'm still working.
~ Will Smith

I sincerely hope that the first section of this book has given you some valuable insight and food for thought. Even though I am basing this information on many of my personal experiences I feel more than qualified to tell you that your work ethic is crucial for many reasons. I will discuss each of these within this section. Resolve to at least think about your work ethic and what it means to you every single day with every thought you think and action you take. If that sounds like a tall order, it is and it's worth it.

Throughout this second section we will explore why the work ethic is so crucial to success in all areas of our lives. Whether or not you will agree with me on this, it is my hope that at least you will revisit your thoughts, actions, and experiences in this area.

On a regular basis I tell my students and clients that there is very little competition in business. This is based on massive research in this field, as well as my personal observations since becoming an online entrepreneur in 2006. Many people will decide to start a business, but few make it past the three month mark.

That's correct. Thousands of people begin a new business or other income generating and producing endeavor each month, yet fewer than five percent of them are willing to stick with it long enough and to do what it takes in order to give themselves even a remote chance at success. I wrote about this phenomenon extensively in my previous book, *Doing What it Takes: The Online Entrepreneur's Playbook*. This won't happen to you because you are still reading and your thinking is slowly beginning to change. Please don't stop reading and thinking now!

Do I Need a Work Ethic?

I am not a product of my circumstances.
I am a product of my decisions.
~ Stephen Covey

I firmly believe that a work ethic is crucial for success. The components of this must be top of mind for you throughout each day, and at some point will become ingrained in your DNA to the point where you will no longer have to actively think about every step you take.

Let's explore how rethinking your current work ethic and choosing to make some changes, mind shifts, and alterations to it will change your personal life, your business, and your perspective as both an entrepreneur and a human being.

As I was outlining this book the phrase "think globally, act locally" came into my mind. I had first heard this back in the 1980s when I was complaining about a co-worker who seemed to only focus on the world view when it came to issues we were discussing and dealing with at our real estate office. He had the "think globally" part down, but was not making the connection as to how he could "act locally" and make an impact on the people and businesses within our community. It was almost as if he believed that nothing he would act upon in our community could ever have an impact on a national or international level. This led to my thinking of this man as a narrow-minded individual who allowed others to make the decisions that we would all need to follow. Nothing any of us said or did would change his mind on this.

Big picture versus small thinking, results, actions, dreams, goals, steps, and strategies comes about as a result of having a work ethic that encompasses more than just yourself. Perhaps I need to discuss this further so that I can make it perfectly clear exactly what I am proposing.

Taking the World View

The idea here is to be able to see the world view on anything you are working to achieve, yet to take action in a way that will affect and change you, your family, and the people closest to you.

For example, politics, religion, and economics rule the world in many ways. So how can you or I have any influence in the outcomes of this global society? As an entrepreneur you can consciously choose to do business in your local community in a way that will serve others living on the other side of our planet. I write books, create training programs, mentor other entrepreneurs on six continents, and speak and present at live conferences, workshops, and other events around the world. I am able to reach and interact with people in many countries because I work online. If I were doing something similar only within the confines of where I live in southern California, my reach would not and could not be nearly as extensive.

This has become so much a part of my work ethic that I no longer have to give much thought to on a daily basis. When someone from Africa or South America or Eastern Europe contacts me to find out more about how I can help them on their entrepreneurial journey I know exactly how to respond to best serve their needs. And if I am not able to assist them personally because I lack the knowledge or experience they are looking for, I am usually able to refer them to a colleague in another part of the world who will be a much better fit.

Belonging to and participating in charities and non-profit organizations has also served me well in this "think globally, act locally" mindset and way of living. As a Rotarian for more than a decade (Rotary is an international service organization, supporting projects such as bringing clean water to third world countries and working tirelessly to eradicate polio from our planet. Their slogan for this year is "People of action.") I have seen firsthand the impact one person can have on someone else in the world. I am also a Zontian. Zonta is a women's business organization that empowers women to become global advocates through service and advocacy.

Their motto is "Achieving global impact through local action." I found that up leveling my work ethic during this past decade has been crucial to my success within these organizations and in my ability to participate fully with their causes and projects.

Another group I am involved in is SEE International. Their Mission is "to provide sustainable medical, surgical, and educational services through volunteer ophthalmic surgeons with the objectives of restoring sight and preventing blindness to disadvantaged individuals worldwide." They are most definitely an example of thinking globally and acting locally in that they regularly offer free eye examinations to people in need within their own city and county, while also reaching the far corners of the earth with their outreach program on six continents and in scores of countries.

Now let's get back to why I believe you need a work ethic to succeed in your daily life. I learned this by observing my own behavior and the behavior and actions of others in the workplace.

My First Property Listing

When I was first working as a real estate agent back in the early 1980s people in my office began telling me that if I wanted help with something to ask the busiest person in the office. This made absolutely no sense to me, as it seemed like the busiest people would already have too much on their plate to take time with helping a new agent such as me. So when I took my first listing and needed help setting up the open house and everything related to that, I went to the two people who always had the time to talk with me.

Leonard had recently retired from a career as an attorney working in the Los Angeles County prosecutor's office. He would tell fascinating stories of cases he had been involved in over the years, including just enough detail for us to figure out who it might be, yet leaving out the names and additional details to protect their privacy. He always had time to go to lunch or to just sit and discuss different aspects of real estate with me or with anyone else who happened to be in the office.

Molly had been working in real estate for more than twenty-five years, but at that time only did it on a part-time basis in order to spend time with her husband, adult children, and two grandchildren.

Her clients loved her because she always made time to help them with anything from moving out of or into another home to setting up appointments for the utilities to be turned on or off. I enjoyed caravanning (the process of looking at new listings when they are first issued) with Molly because we took our time and discussed both the flaws and the merits of each property we saw on that day.

I asked the two of them to help me get ready for my upcoming open house for my brand new listing. It was five days away and I knew there must be a ton of things to do that I had no idea about right then. And I was a little bit nervous, so it was likely I was forgetting something very important.

That morning I also saw Olga, undeniably the busiest person in the office. She had always made sure to look me in the eye, shake my hand, and ask me if I needed anything each time I saw her, but I knew she was busy with her own transactions and probably didn't want to take her valuable time to help me with something so trivial. So on that particular day I smiled, thanked her for her offer of help, and went on my way.

Just a side note here: I should never have assumed she was too busy or unwilling to help out a new person. It would have been so much better if I had taken her at her word when she offered her help. This was simply the story I created at that time around this situation.

Leonard and Molly happily agreed to help me and I graciously accepted their offer. We began at once, discussing all kinds of things. Looking back, we did a lot more talking and discussing different options that we did in actually making a workable plan.

So the day came when my open house would occur. It was a Sunday morning, and I first stopped at the local convenience store to pick up the Sunday newspaper. I wanted to take it with me to my listing to look through while I was hosting my open house. Then I stopped at three different intersections to place my signs in the ground so that people driving by would see the name of my company, the address, and the hours of the open house.

The owner was waiting for me when I arrived around eleven o'clock. He was going to leave for several hours to make it more comfortable for the potential buyers to walk through his house, to comment, and to ask me questions about his home. I walked him out to his car and then went back inside to set up a little table with my flyers and to do my own walk through the house to see if anything needed to be done, like closing a closet door or flushing a toilet. I knew enough from my limited time in real estate to understand that the little things mattered. I also carefully spread out the piece of foil I had in my purse, sprinkled a few drops of vanilla on it, and placed it strategically on the center rack in the over at 250°. It was supposed to smell like someone was baking, giving the entire house an aroma of the perfect family home. Then I opened the real estate section of the Sunday paper to see how my advertisement had turned out.

I pulled that section out first and separated it from the rest of the bulky newspaper. Then I got caught up with the front page news and the entertainment section before I glanced at my watch and saw that it was already past noon and no one had come by to see the house. So I quickly opened the real estate section to locate my advertisement.

I scanned each page, slowly at first and then frantically to locate the information on my open house. It wasn't long before I realized that my advertisement had not made it into the newspaper at all. I thought back to the events of the previous few days and tried to reenact it in my mind. The deadline to place an ad into the Sunday edition of the real estate section was on Wednesday at noon. Leonard had read over my copy and deemed in worthy of publication. So what could have happened?

Eventually about a dozen people did attend my open house, having seen my signs throughout the neighborhood. Many of these were neighbors and a few were actually good prospects for this home. But I was livid when I thought about the hundred or so people I would have met during those five hours if the ad had run in the newspaper as planned.

When I got back to the office that afternoon Leonard was not around but Molly was sitting at her desk reading the newspaper. Her radio was playing some popular music and I recognized Robert Palmer and his song "Addicted to Love."

I couldn't resist the irony as I asked her if she had seen any interesting open houses listed in the real estate section. She paused for a moment before reacting. Then her face became red and she jumped up out of her chair like a fire had been lit beneath her.

It turned out that Leonard had asked her to place the ad for me on Wednesday and she had completely forgotten about it until this exact moment.

I was still angry, hurt, and disappointed over what had occurred and I asked her if she had written it down anywhere. Within a few minutes I realized I had asked the wrong people to help me. Molly and Leonard were not taking their real estate businesses seriously and their actions and results proved it. It would have been much better for me to have asked Olga to help me because she was making things happen in her business. The busiest person in the office was busy for good reason. And on that day I learned a lesson that did not hit me hard until many years later. The lesson was that people with a strong and thoughtful work ethic are the ones to spend time with, to learn from, to emulate, and to ask for help. For they are the ones who will make a difference in the world on a day to day basis.

The following week I met with Olga and she and I outlined some activities and a strategy that would keep me on track as a new real estate agent. She never mentioned what had happened with Molly and Leonard, and I appreciated that very much.

You might be thinking that this experience would have been enough for me to realize how important developing and maintaining a strong work ethic would be to my own success over the coming years. But back then I was still in the mode of looking outward for the answers I was seeking, instead of reflecting from within. In other words, I placed blame on other people for what was happening in my own life instead of accepting full responsibility and understanding that my life and my success depended entirely upon my actions, beliefs, values, and commitment to guiding the situations and circumstances I was encountering in the direction that would be best not only for me, but for others as well. It's the kind of win-win philosophy embodied by those who "get it".

In addition to the lesson I mentioned above, I also learned that I must take full responsibility for anything and everything that enters into my realm of consciousness, not just the situations I am directly involved with. I'll share more about this concept and thought process later on. It just took me another two decades to implement this line of thinking into my daily life. It won't take you this long because you are in the right place at the right time as you read this book.

Doing What You Think You Cannot Do

You must be willing to do the things
you think you cannot do.
~ Eleanor Roosevelt

Rethinking your work ethic will give you a new lease on your life. There will be a noticeable spring in your step, a sparkle in your eye, and a chuckle always at the ready on your lips. You will be transformed with this process.

There are so many things I now do regularly which I thought I could not ever do. I am reminded of something motivational speaker and business trainer Brian Tracy taught me when I was fortunate enough to spend several days with him in a small group setting in Palm Springs, California during 2006. Brian said "Everything in business is a learnable skill. Decide what it is you need to learn and then learn how to do it or delegate the task or activity to someone else who already has that skill." These words changed my life as I realized I did not need to have some intuitive skills or be born with a mind for marketing in order to be a successful entrepreneur.

Now I will share with you some of the things I have now done and accomplished that I once thought I could not do.

Becoming a Published Author

Even though I spend time writing every single day, it is not the same as making the time in my schedule to write a book. As I began to rethink my work ethic a decade ago, I knew it would be a struggle to turn myself into a writer. But I was willing to embrace this struggle and to start writing on a daily basis to improve my skills in this area.

It began with my writing two hundred and fifty word articles to submit to the article directory sites. I turned many of these into blog posts, and for my other niche blogs I would also write two to three hundred word posts on various topics.

The writing was awful, if I do say so myself. Each day that I published another article or post I was in fear that someone from my previous life would find it, read it, and share it with others. My fear was that these people, none of whom I knew any longer, would read my writing aloud and laugh hysterically at how poorly it was written. I imagined them saying something like "No wonder the children in America are having trouble with school; they have teachers who can hardly put a paragraph together properly."

But I persevered and thought about how amazing it would be if I could someday write and publish an entire book. And I kept hearing the phrase "How do you eat an elephant? One bite at a time." in my head. Could it be possible to write bite-sized chunks over time and somehow piece them all together into a full length book?

Time went on and my book was still not any closer to being written than it had been when I first decided that I wanted to become a published author. In January of 2010 I was in Las Vegas meeting with my Mastermind group. At some point I mentioned to my dear friend and colleague Dr. Jeanette Cates that I wanted to write my book but just couldn't afford to take three months away from my business in order to do this. She then said something that would change my life forever. It went something like this:

"Why on earth would you take three months away from your business to write a book? Just write for an hour or so each day and it will be finished before you know it."

I was speechless at the simplicity of what she was suggesting. But Jeanette was correct and in June of 2010 my first book was published. I have refined my process somewhat since that time, but as I write this fifteenth book I was tell you that I still write for an hour or ninety minutes each day and complete each book within about six weeks from start to finish.

Becoming a Public Speaker

It is said that people fear speaking in public almost as much as their impending death. How is this possible? Isn't this way too dramatic a statement?

This was true for me for more than fifty years of my life. Speaking in front of my classroom of students for twenty years was never an issue for me. Even in front of several hundred students in the auditorium I was quite effective in teaching, persuading, and encouraging young people of all ages. But once I was in front of even a small group of adults I would become frozen with fear.

One time I was asked to do a presentation for my fellow teachers at a staff meeting. Arriving early to set up the overhead projector I was gripped with fear and anxiety. The teachers began to file into the room and I had to begin. They were talking to one another noisily and throwing me off completely from what I had planned to say to them at the beginning.

Not able to remember anything and awkwardly shuffling through my notes and overhead transparencies, I asked them to count off "one, two, three, four" to get their attention. This settled them down until one of the teachers asked me why we were doing this. I answered that it was to get their attention and I lost all credibility with them on that day.

I limped through my presentation, the assistant principal moved on to the next item on the agenda, and I had once again failed as a public speaker.

Fast forward to 2006, when I had resigned from my teaching job and had given away my best real estate clients. I was sitting at a Rotary Club meeting at lunch and the President began passing the microphone to the people who were involved with some of their ongoing projects. As it came closer to my turn I began to get flushed and my stomach started to ache. It was three people away from me, and then two people away, and then everything went dark and I felt the person next to me squeezing the cold microphone into my clammy hands.

I don't remember the words I mumbled into the microphone that day, but the way I felt at that moment will stay with me forever. I was like a little child separated from its mother in a crowded place, so afraid and not capable of helping themselves back to safety. Someone next to me on the other side gently took the microphone out of my hands and at that moment I felt small and very alone. For the next few minutes I couldn't see or hear anything and soon the feeling began to come back into my body. I promised myself that I would never allow anyone to put me into that awkward and uncomfortable position again.

But over the next few weeks my thoughts began to go to the opposite end of that spectrum. What if I could learn to speak in front of groups? Was that even a possibility for me?

I thought about the speakers I had heard over the years who had truly moved me with their words and message. I thought about the President of the Rotary Club, the other club members who spoke regularly, and about the weekly guest speakers who shared so much with us. Were these people so different from me?

It took my mind quite a while to process these new thoughts and feelings, leading to a progression that brought me new insight about who I was deep down inside. I thought back to a speech class I was required to take in the seventh grade, and how I had experienced the same feelings of self-doubt and physical pain, and how the only time this had not been the case was when I did a speech on how to create Christmas ornaments using egg cartons, glitter, and string. I had actually enjoyed giving that presentation in front of the other kids in my class.

Perhaps I was on to something. When I could show the audience something while I was speaking to take the focus off of myself, at least partially, then speaking was not so painful.

The very next time I was asked to speak I created a two page handout to share with the audience. It was actually one page front and back and contained tips on getting started with social media, as well as my contact information. Most of the people continued to look at me while I spoke, but having even a few glance down at the handout made me much more comfortable being in front of them. And I kept a copy of the handout in my hands, referring to items on it from time to time.

Over the next year I was asked to speak at several events, and once my first book was published many people began to ask me to speak to their audience on the topics of online marketing, building a responsive list, and getting started as an online entrepreneur. I continued to be extremely anxious and uncomfortable in front of audiences, but forced myself to speak anyway.

It was when I was speaking to a group of about five hundred entrepreneurs in Minneapolis, Minnesota in June of 2010 that everything changed for me in terms of public speaking. My topic was affiliate marketing and my PowerPoint was as complete as possible as I began my presentation. I was quite nervous, so I drank some water, used the restroom, and went on stage.

Then I saw that I had left something out of one of the slides and began to panic. I wasn't sure if I should mention it or just keep my fingers crossed they wouldn't notice it and carry on. But I decided to tell them about the mistake and when I did a few people in the audience laughed.

That was a turning point for me. I made another funny comment and then went on with my talk. As I looked out into the audience I was poised and confident, and right then I promised myself to always remember that moment. Being able to have fun with the audience while sharing my information felt good, and now I am able to do that each time I speak. I'm also able to sell my products and services quite effectively from the stage, a skill that continues to earn me lots of additional income.

None of this would have been possible if I hadn't pursued speaking as something I thought I could not do.

If you are just getting started as a speaker I will recommend that you get some assistance with this. Toastmasters was not a good fit for me for several reasons, so I contacted an acting coach who had worked with entrepreneurs and people in the corporate world who were required to speak in person to groups and to have an impact on a regular basis.

Over a four month period I made the drive into Los Angeles twice a week to meet with a group of aspiring actors and some who were already working actors. We covered a variety of areas and I enjoyed the exercises and activities immensely. It was a combination of mental, psychological, and physical things that I needed to bring into alignment in order for my speaking to become more natural.

After being involved with this training for a month or so the acting coach called me and said I would be perfect for a role they were casting in a movie. Not wanting to give up my new life in favor of a life in film I respectfully declined. My friends still tease me about it to this day. I never did find out what the role was for exactly, but I smile when I think of myself as the "reluctant movie star".

Driving Across the United States...Alone!

Long ago my family and I used to drive across the country on a regular basis. Whether we were taking a vacation, visiting other family members, or going to a new location where my husband could find work, driving to get from one location to another was a part of our lives. We would pack everything we needed and hit the road.

There were some good reasons for this, namely cost and convenience. This all began in the 1970s and we could not afford to fly even part of the way across the country at that time. And even if we had somehow scraped the money together for airplane tickets we would have still needed to rent a car when we arrived. No, we were not in a financial position to do this, and with young children along it just made sense to drive. There was even a jingle for this - "See the U.S.A. in your Chevrolet." Do you remember seeing that on television with Dinah Shore singing the song?

But I digress. During the 1970s and 1980s we drove back and forth across the United States many, many times. And then it all ended because all of our lives had changed. Over the years I would still drive from southern California to the San Francisco Bay area, or to San Diego or Las Vegas, but it wasn't until 2015 that I seriously thought about making a cross country road trip on my own.

It was at my Weekend Marketer Live event and workshop in Los Angeles in the spring of 2015 that I first spoke about it out loud. At some point in my presentation I announced to the audience that I would be driving across the country that summer and planned on stopping to see as many of my clients as I could during that trip.

Well, my people looked stunned but no one said anything. The next day one person came up to me privately to ask me if I was seriously considering taking this road trip. I answered that I was indeed. But it wasn't mentioned again, and when I got home from that event and looked at a map and the logistics of attempting to visit people in so many locations scattered across our huge country I almost let it go.

Almost.

Then I looked at the map again and thought about flying to three different cities, renting a car in each one, and then driving to see one or more of my clients before heading back to the airport for the next leg of the trip.

At some point I lost my enthusiasm for this venture and no longer had a mental commitment to seeing it through. My clients had not seemed that excited at the prospect of me descending upon them in their community and once I had let the idea go it was gone. I honestly did not give it another thought until one year later.

Once again I was standing at the front of the conference room in Los Angeles for my Weekend Marketer Live event and workshop. It was now March of 2016 and many of my same clients were in attendance, along with some new ones. And at some point over that weekend I heard my voice speaking to announce that this was the year my road trip would actually happen. Was that me talking?

I had just published my fourteenth book, *Doing What It Takes - The Online Entrepreneur's Playbook* and I was anxious to do whatever it would take to make all of my goals a successful reality. And this was coming across in my words and tone as I spoke to the group. They sat up in the chairs and made eye contact. They believed me this time.

Less than three months later my car was packed and I was on my way. I would cover more than six thousand miles over a twenty-one day road trip, driving through seventeen states and visiting more than a dozen people, including clients, students, family, and friends.

As I drove out of my city and on to the open road headed northeast, I just knew this would be a worthwhile adventure to share for many years to come.

My first visit was to be with Hans, a Chinese fellow who had been our exchange student eight years previous. We had kept in touch with him and even spent time with him over the years. He was now a law student at Washington University in St. Louis, Missouri and was excited that I would be spending a day and a half with him. My trip was well planned, so I knew fairly closely on what day I would arrive at his house. His roommate was in China for the summer so there was plenty of room for me.

My drive was going along smoothly, and except for my back being a little sore I was enjoying the drive and staying right on track according to my plan. Being out on the open roads suited me, and the fact that I was alone meant that I had lots of time to think. I stayed at motels on the first and second nights of my trip and was scheduled to arrive in St. Louis in the late afternoon on the third day.

By the time I had exited the freeway to head towards Hans' house my back and legs were very sore. I was ready for him to prepare a traditional Chinese dinner for us, to be able to jump in for a hot shower, and then get to bed early so he and I could see some sights the next day. It didn't quite work out this way.

When I pulled up in front of his house and realized that he lived on the upper floor I knew I was in trouble. Carefully extricating myself from the driver's seat I found that the feeling was all but gone from my left leg. And my back hurt more than I could ever remember.

I was in deep trouble.

Again I took a look at the gorgeous two-story brick building that Hans had called home for the past year. I fixed my gaze on the large plate glass window at the top and then I saw the handsome smiling face of Hans looking down at me.

I would love to tell you that we spent the following couple of days laughing and reminiscing, visiting the newly remodeled St. Louis Gateway Arch, and eating his incredible Chinese dishes, but that was not to be.

My pain was severe and I was crippled when I got out of the car. So off to the nearest urgent care I went, and they immediately transferred me to the local hospital. Within a few hours the orthopedic surgeon and his team had encircled me, and he recommended that I fly back to Los Angeles in the morning and make arrangements for my car to be picked up.

At this point in my life I no longer entertain the thought of giving up for even a nanosecond, especially in a situation such as this one. Instead, I thanked him and the others for their help and by the next morning I was driving away from St. Louis, through Illinois, and on to Kentucky to resume my road trip and schedule.

What transpired during this twenty-one day journey was nothing short of miraculous and I wouldn't have traded the experience for anything in the world. Even with this mishap I was able to keep to my schedule and returned to California within twelve hours of when I had initially planned. I did make it through all seventeen states and visited more than a dozen clients, students, family, and friends along the way. Yes, it was physically painful most of the time, but that seemed minor in comparison to what I was able to add to my list of life experiences and joy.

One Day at a Time

You may be wondering right about now why I have shared these particular stories with you in this chapter. The primary reason is to share a concept with you that hopefully will have a powerful impact upon how you think about or rethink your work effort. This concept is that we can never see the entire picture at the beginning of a journey and that we must move forward anyway, trusting and having faith that each small step is meant to draw us closer to our goal or destination, even if it sometimes seems that we are taking two steps backward before we can take even one more step forward. Please allow me to explain what I mean here.

When I was first diagnosed with breast cancer in 1992 I was terrified of what would unfold during this process. I had so many questions. Could they perform a lumpectomy and save most of my breast? Would I need chemotherapy? Would I lose my hair? Would I need to quit my job? How would my family and friends react to this news? Would I live through this?

If the doctors and surgeons would have spelled out exactly what I was likely to go through during the next year it would have been too much for me to hear and take in. They were experienced enough to know this and spared me the gory details of what was in store for me as I fought for my life. Instead, they unfolded my experience in smaller chunks. We discussed the next procedure, the next operation, the next day or two.

Even though they could see the bigger picture there was no need for me to think that far down the road. Just as I trusted my maps and navigation system to get me from one city to the next during my road map, the doctors helped me to navigate the medical system and the procedures one day or week to the next. The results in this case were life and death, so anything connected to your personal life and business is typically not nearly as dramatic.

And the final thought I wish to leave you with when it comes to being willing to do what you think right now you cannot do is this: Not feeling like it is no excuse!

In life we either have reasons or results, so if you find that you do not feel like doing something, do it anyway and keep moving forward towards the activities you do want to engage in as a part of your daily life.

Those Who Live This Way

*Talent is cheaper than table salt. What separates the
talented person from the successful one is lots of hard work.*
~ Stephen King

You may have been raised in a family that stressed a strong and
ongoing work ethic from the time you were a small child. If so, then
you have a decided and distinct edge and advantage over someone
like myself. But this will never keep me from doing everything within
my power to keep up or to even surpass your efforts when it comes
to achieving my goals.

Being willing to do the work allows me to play on a level field
with anyone I encounter. It doesn't matter to me if they are smarter,
more talented, better connected, or more highly educated. My work
ethic speaks for itself when it comes to my ongoing high performance
as an author, entrepreneur, and human being. But I am most
certainly not unique with this way of living life each day. Let's
discuss some more notable people who exemplify the work ethic in
action.

Will Smith is the first person who comes to mind when I think
about someone with what he refers to as a "ridiculous, sickening"
work ethic. In fact, this is what he has to say on this topic of work
ethic:

"I've never really viewed myself as particularly talented. I've
viewed myself as slightly above average in talent. And where I excel
is ridiculous, sickening, work ethic. You know, while the other guy's
sleeping? I'm working. While the other guy's eatin'? I'm working."

Will defines himself as an actor, producer, rapper, and songwriter,
and I will add the label "motivational speaker" to his resume. You
may remember him as a rapper known as The Fresh Prince during

the 1980s or as a fledgling actor in the television situation comedy *The Fresh Prince of Bel Air* beginning in 1990, or perhaps you were not aware of Will Smith until he starred in his first film in 1993, *Six Degrees of Separation*.

You can Google him to learn more, but the bottom line is that Will has been able to achieve what most people choose not to even go after because of a work ethic instilled in him and his siblings by his father while he was a young boy.

One summer his father took him and his younger brother Harry to a building he owned in Philadelphia and told them they were to rebuild the brick wall. They told him that this task was impossible, but his father said he did not ever want them to think of something as being impossible to achieve. It took Will and Harry a year, but they did rebuild that wall one brick and glob of mortar at a time. And that's when he understood an important principle that he still teaches today. And that is to not think of it as rebuilding a brick wall, but to instead think of the project as laying one brick at a time in the best way you possibly can.

When it comes to making it in Hollywood as an actor, Will says: "The separation of talent and skill is one of the greatest misunderstood concepts for people who are trying to excel, who have dreams, who want to do things. Talent you have naturally. Skill is only developed by hours and hours and hours of beating on your craft."

And I'll leave you with what he has to say about how he is willing to "die on a treadmill." If someone challenges him to outlast them on a treadmill, only two things can happen. Either the other person will give up or he will die.

Will doesn't care if someone is smarter, or stronger, or more talented than he is; he is willing to outwork anyone and everyone so that his dreams and goals can come to fruition.

Mark Cuban

I find the life story of Mark Cuban to be an interesting and insightful one. His paternal grandfather immigrated to the United States through Ellis Island from Russia in the 1890s and made his living by selling various types of merchandise out of the back of a truck. His father worked for more than fifty years in a car upholstery shop.

In addition to being exposed from a young age to hard working family members who exhibited a strong work ethic, Mark became an early follower of author and philosopher Ayn Rand's work. This brought about a change in his thinking, guiding him towards a belief system where he would think as an individual, take risks to reach his goals, and take full responsibility for his successes and failures.

In 2000 he purchased a majority stake in the NBA (National Basketball Association) team the Dallas Mavericks, purchasing them from H. Ross Perot Jr. for two hundred eighty-five million dollars. The Mavericks are considered by Forbes magazine to be the ninth most valuable basketball franchise in the NBA. I will let you do the research to learn more about Cuban's other endeavors, but suffice it to say that he has been a thought leader and action taker as an entrepreneur for many decades and is an icon when it comes to rethinking the work ethic every single day. And I love one of his quotes, "Perfection is the enemy of profitability."

Oprah Winfrey

Oprah was born to a single, teenaged mother on a farm in rural Mississippi, and later sent to Tennessee to live with a man she refers to her father. As a child she was forced to wear dresses made out of potato sacks, and was hit with a stick if she misbehaved or didn't complete her chores properly. Despite this humble upbringing Oprah has gone on to become a great person, admired by people all over the world.

I can remember first hearing about her from a friend who had relocated to California from Chicago. She had a large poster of Oprah hanging in her office and when I asked who this was she went on to rave about all of Oprah's accomplishments. This was in 1985, so you can imagine how little she had achieved by that time, in comparison to what she would go on to do in her life over these next three decades.

What struck me at the time was that no matter that she was an African-American woman raised in poverty, Oprah was willing to do whatever it would take to succeed. Being taught to read at age three by her grandmother, who also had her speaking to the congregation at church on a regular basis and later being sent to live with her father, who insisted that her education be given top priority were influencing factors that shaped her young life.

While in high school she joined the speech team and won oratory contests sponsored by the local Elk's Lodge (a group I am proud to have been a part of for over a decade now), providing the opportunity to go to college on a full scholarship. I believe that looking back at what you enjoyed and excelled in during your formative years is excellent insight into what you might be interested in and have an affinity for later on in your life.

How do the beliefs, values, and actions of the people I have shared with you here come into play with what you wish to achieve in your own life? Think about this for now and we will revisit this in the Action Steps section.

Part II Action Steps

I offered up the quote from Eleanor Roosevelt early in this section. It goes like this:

> *You must be willing to do the things*
> *you think you cannot do.*

Think about and make a list of the things you think you cannot do but wish to accomplish while you are still alive. Do not base your list on what you might consider to be "realistic", but instead allow your mind to be freed up as you daydream the possibilities. I will continue to believe that anything is possible for us, no matter what restrictions you and I may have subconsciously allowed into our hearts and minds over time.

My examples included wanting to write a book, to become a public speaker, and to drive across the United States and back by myself. This year I will add to this with even more personal and business goals that are meaningful to me.

Be sure to include the "why" around any of your goals that you may now consider to be an impossibility.

Thinking Globally While Acting Locally

Can you personally think of a person, company, or organization that demonstrates the concept of "thinking globally while acting locally"? If so, write down your thoughts and perceptions of what they are doing to make the world a better place. Does it require a strong work ethic to achieve this level of performance in their chosen field.

If you cannot or are unable to think of an example of this in your community, seek out the people and groups that might fall into this category. I will promise you that in your research you will encounter people who are continuing to rethink the work ethic as they challenge themselves to do more each day.

People With a Strong Work Ethic

So, how do the beliefs, values, and actions of the people I have shared with you in this section come into play with what you wish to achieve in your own life?

Have you ever had the experience of being let down or disappointed by someone who did not follow through with what they said they would do? Did you think of this behavior as having anything to do with that person's work ethic, or was it something else? Write down your thoughts and experiences around this.

What did you take away from reading about people who demonstrate and model a strong work ethic in their lives every single day? Watch some of the videos from Will Smith on this topic and write down your thoughts as they occur.

Can there be such a thing as too strong a work ethic, leading to becoming a workaholic, or some other issues in one's life such as those related to maintaining relationships?

Are you taking full and complete responsibility for everything that occurs in your life, even if it seems to be outside of the areas you should be responsible for?

Part III – What If You Rethink Your Work Ethic?

I never feared about my skills because I put in the work. Work ethic eliminates fear.
So if you put forth the work, what are you fearing?
You know what you're capable of doing and what you're not.
~ Michael Jordan

Earlier I promised you that rethinking your work ethic will give you a new lease on your life. I mentioned a noticeable spring in your step, a sparkle in your eye, a smile playing on your lips, and a chuckle always at the ready in your throat. Is this in process as you read further? Yes, the people around you each day, as well as those who are meeting you for the first time or those who haven't spent time with you recently will all observe the profound difference in this "new you."

It's about a new level of confidence, a topic I wrote about extensively and almost exclusively in *The Inner Game of Internet Marketing*, co-authored with the late Geoff Hoff. Having confidence is like holding a winning lottery ticket in your pocket, yet far superior to that experience because you can control this aspect of your life completely on your own.

During this next section I would like for you to sit comfortably and imagine the possibilities of a life on your terms. Visualize what your life would be like if you were willing to embrace the struggle of moving to the next level in your life and working each day to exceed your highest potential.

Think back to a time in your life when you wholeheartedly knew and believed that anything was possible. What did that look like, feel like, taste like all those years ago? Remember as much detail as you can about those days when no one and no situation could deter you from your dreams. Back then you were not willing to settle for anything less than what you wanted.

Those days have returned to your life experience. Just do the work and the world will once again become your oyster.

What if the simple yet powerful steps outlined within these pages enabled you to do, be, and have more in your life than you ever thought possible? Read on as we continue the journey of rethinking your work ethic, embracing any and all struggles you will encounter, and exceeding your own potential in a way that will move mountains.

How Will Your Life Be Different Now?

Life shrinks or expands in proportion to one's courage.
~ Anais Nin

Change of any type can be scary. And if you are anything like me you will be more comfortable staying in the safe place you have created for yourself than by purposely venturing into unchartered territory. But I am here to tell you that leveling up and becoming a person who is not only capable, but one whom is actually going after a higher level performance type of existence is worthwhile for so many reasons. Hopefully, you have already had one or more of these experiences during your lifetime.

Having this type of courage to move far away from your comfort zone and into a life that demands a stronger and more focused work ethic is simple, but most definitely not easy. I continue to seek out the people, situations, and opportunities for expansion in my own thinking, actions, and behavior. Remember that our goal for doing this is to lead us to changing our nature and making our new habits stick and evolve over time.

We all did this as children. The baby literally steps out of their comfort zone as they take their first step. We all had the courage to practice feeding and dressing ourselves, to fall off of the bicycle multiple times, and to mispronounce a simple word as we read our book report aloud in front of the class. We were more than willing to skin our knees and to look foolish at times in order to achieve our goals. If you think of it this way, it's difficult to imagine anything we do as adults being any more frightening.

My journey has been a fascinating one because I became wide-eyed and filled with hope at the prospect of being able to change my life completely as a result of my own actions. I was much like a young child, trusting in those around me to guide me in the direction that would be right specifically for me. My only challenge, in the beginning, was in finding these people who had walked this path and were knowledgeable and caring about helping me to make the shifts in my current way of thinking, taking action, adjusting my attitude, and changing my behavior on my way to changing my nature.

Asking For Help

Most of us are not very practiced in the art of asking for help. I know I wasn't, and somewhere along the way I had picked up the habit of believing that asking someone else for any type of help or assistance was an indicator of my weakness and of imminent failure. What a silly notion that is, and I regret that it took me so many years to figure out this simple truth about the power of asking for help.

So when I was ready to begin my journey to live a different life from the one I had been living for decades, I turned to the people around me and asked for their help. They responded positively to my request and I was on my way. In fact, they were actually relieved that I was finally including them on my journey and would be open-minded and willing to take action on their suggestions.

This began innocently enough, and soon escalated to a full force attempt on my part to achieve the goals and dreams I had long ago forgotten. I was determined to make up for lost time and to make at least some type of a difference in the world.

The year was 2005 and a woman I knew and respected introduced me to a couple she thought I would enjoy getting to know. She arranged a get together at her home one evening and we were all invited. It was there that I met a couple who were living a life most people could not even imagine. Talk about courageous!

They had started out as many couples do, finishing college, pursuing their chosen careers, and starting a family. But somewhere along the way they had become disillusioned with the life they had planned were living and yearned to do something else. Fortunately, they came to this realization almost simultaneously, making the next part of their journey even more meaningful and poignant for them as a couple.

After a lengthy discussion with their young adult children and some research into the possibilities that were of interest to them, this couple decided to change their life completely. They quite their corporate jobs, sold their suburban home, and moved to the quiet countryside they had visited regularly over the past twenty-five years.

The new house was less than a quarter of the size of their previous home, so it was necessary to sell or give away many of their material possessions. They also decided to drastically change their eating habits, giving up most meat, dairy products, and processed food in the process. When I first visited their home they threw open the kitchen cabinets and then the refrigerator to show me the bare necessities they kept on hand. Then they blended a green drink and poured me a glass. I drank it, but it was an acquired taste, to be sure.

It wasn't as though they had become new-age hippies living off the land. No, it was almost the opposite of that as they began to renew and rejuvenate their lives by starting over and learning more about everything they had ever found to be of interest. They both wanted a fresh start and were willing to do whatever was necessary in order to get there.

Over the course of the next six months I spent as much time with these new friends as I possibly could. What began as voyeurism on my part evolved and morphed into a friendship of mass proportions. Like a human sponge I soaked up as much knowledge and information as I could and offered to share with them anything that could be of interest in their new venture.

I've been in real estate since 1983 and this area was of great interest to them at the time. We discussed investment strategies and they pulled information and knowledge out of me that I had either long forgotten or had filed in my brain as being of little interest to others. They showed me that I had great potential in so many areas and encouraged me to follow my heart, along with my mind as I made changes to my own life.

And most importantly to me at that time in my life, my new friends taught me that asking for help was indeed a noble endeavor.

If you are ready to rethink your work ethic, connecting with the people who are excited to help you is crucial to your success. Lest you think this is not for you and that you would prefer to be self-reliant, know that historically the people and groups who embraced that phrase - self-reliance - to describe their life strategy have almost always become those who were most dependent upon others for their very survival.

Instead, be willing to take your journey alongside those who also want to live a life of purposeful meaning and joy. Spending time with like-minded individuals will accelerate your progress. I knew I was ready back in 2005 and like Maya Angelou said "...wouldn't take nothing for my journey now."

Perhaps you are in a similar place in your life right now. You know that there is more of something you desire available to you, but you might not be sure what that is exactly and how to best pursue it. If this describes the feelings you are experiencing, please know that by rethinking your current work ethic, embracing the struggles that are bound to come up as you do, and knowing that you can and will exceed your own potential is not only possible but highly probable. We are all humans in the process of becoming who we are to become, and not one of us will reach our destination while still walking the earth. Once you relax into that reality everything will open up for you very quickly.

Is It Time to Rethink Your Own Work Ethic?

Not long ago I had lunch with a woman who was describing her teenage son as being someone with a strong work ethic based on his enthusiasm in completing a project he had decided to take on recently. Others at the table did a face palm and couldn't make eye contact with her as she spoke about how this young man had gone all out to do his very best during this period of time. I refer to this as "situational work ethic", which is a very different trait than what I am discussing here.

I would venture to say that all of us exhibit the type of energy and focus her son had when faced with something we truly want to achieve. In my own life I worked hard to achieve a number of goals, including but not limited to graduating from UCLA with honors, purchasing my first home, being accepted at the law school of my choice, landing a specific job I wanted, and working towards my teaching credential. But I achieved each of these goals in fits and spurts, meaning that I was unable to maintain this focus, clarity, and enthusiasm over extended periods of time.

For example, while I was an undergraduate at UCLA I considered quitting on multiple occasions. The work load was too intense for my liking, and when I did not perform up to my own or the school's expectations, or when I was asked to do something that took me out of my comfort zone I was ready to leave it all behind. It was only because the consequences would have been too great that I was willing to tough it out and move forward. I even managed to graduate Cum Laude because I worked hard during my senior year and raised my grade point average.

The same was true with other events in my life. I sought to avoid the pain of failure and defeat rather than to pursue the satisfaction and pleasure that could arise after working hard consistently.

But during all of these years no one would have ever accused me of being someone with a strong work ethic. No, I was someone who picked and chose the projects I would participate in at a higher level. And just as the teenage boy I have mentioned, I was regularly let down by my own inaction and inability to follow through with enthusiasm and interest. In later years I even began to refer to myself as being lazy, even though I was able to accomplish many tasks that moved my life forward. I no longer describe myself in this way because every day I wake up with an action-based to-do list and specific goals to work on and complete.

Rethinking my own work ethic made me finally understand that it would be necessary for me to work hard each day in order to achieve the level of success I felt that I craved and deserved. Once I discovered this I realized that it leveled the playing field when it came to most things in life and in business. If we only need to work hard as a starting point then it is simple to rise above the competition and make a name for ourselves in the process.

After reading this far you may be wondering what will change initially in your life that you will become aware of consciously. I will warn you that you may become impatient with people around you who continue to complain and not even make an effort to live up to, let alone exceed their potential. When you first have this experience you will wonder what has happened and who you have become.

Then you will slide comfortably into the role of a person who will never have to settle for less than you want and expect for the remainder of your life.

Know that having the courage to expand your life in this way is not commonplace. It sets you apart from others and positions you as a thought leader among your peers. Deciding to embark on this journey may also, at least temporarily distance you from some of the people who are dominant in your life right now and may cause a rift in your relationship. And also understand that this is a part of the process and it will work itself out in time. Take some time to think about all of this before going on to the next chapter.

Seeing Life and Business in a New Light

We owe you everything. You trusted us. You showed up. You tolerated our impact on your world, even when you didn't invite us in.
~ Seth Godin

Have you ever had the experience of finally seeing a situation differently than you had ever thought possible? What I mean by this is that over time, or with new information you can sometimes have a completely revised view of and perspective on something in your life.

For example, as an elementary school teacher I viewed my school campus as the center of the universe for myself and my students. After teaching on this campus for six years I moved on to another school that was different in every possible way. For one thing, my former school had about five hundred students, and we were on a traditional school calendar of being in class from early September through the middle of June each year. My new school had more than two thousand students and ran year-round with four separate tracks.

This meant that five hundred students were always on vacation, another five hundred were just returning, five hundred more were on their way to vacation, and a thousand students were ongoing. I was assigned to "C" Track at this school. We began on the first weekday of July each year, went off track after six weeks around the end of August, returned from our first vacation at the beginning of October, went on our second vacation at the beginning of March, and returned in the middle of April to complete our school year at the end of June. Yes, it's exhausting just writing it here so you can imagine what it was like to live through this experience year in and year out.

When I returned to my previous school for a visit during that first September at the new one I was amazed at the calm atmosphere. Everything appeared smaller to me, and both the adults and the students seemed like they were moving about in slow motion compared to those at my new school. Nothing had changed, except for my perspective.

Over time and under certain circumstances this will be the experience in your life and business I am referring to here. When you begin to step up your work ethic you may go from seeing things that occur as being simply "transactional" to seeing them as being more "relational" and a part of a much larger picture.

I will give you an example here based on my online business. A woman I have great respect for as a writer and entrepreneur recently launched a new course on marketing with email. The content was superb and she asked me to promote this training to my community. After reviewing her work for a second time I decided not to recommend it and here is my reason why.

She was launching this new email marketing course on a platform where everything is seen and perceived as being transactional. People purchase at a very low price and many do not even read and consume the product they buy, let alone use it to build and grow their own businesses. The perception is that the price is low because the value of the content is not great enough to warrant a different attitude or expectation from the buyer. These buyers tend to know very little about the vendors in this scenario.

If this woman had launched this new course on her own platform everything could have been very different. The price should have been, in my humble, yet experienced opinion about ten times as much as she was selling it for, and the sales she would have made would have led to much greater things for her over time. This also makes the product more attractive to affiliates who can help to change your business and your bottom line practically overnight. These buyers would not only have known her name, they would have also become quite interested in her and in everything else she is doing online. This is because these sales would have been more relational in nature.

There is a saying that no sale is ever final. I have always said that a sale of any one of my books, products, or training courses is just the beginning of my relationship with the buyer. I want their expectations to be so great that I need to continue to level up my game to keep up with what they want and deserve from me.

Can you imagine selling your products and services for one tenth of their value to keep you from having to do more than the bare minimum? Or, to phrase this in reverse, can you imagine earning ten times as much and having the opportunity to take your business to the next level by simply engaging with your clients and customers and building and nurturing a relationship with those who purchase from you? Definitely something to think about, yes?

Push or Pull Strategy - the Marketing Conundrum

The Seth Godin quote at the beginning of this chapter brings me to this next topic for entrepreneurs wanting to rethink their work ethic and to see their life and business in a new light. If you are not familiar with Seth, he is a thought leader and almost a household name in the areas of marketing and business and has shaped the thinking of many people such as myself over the years.

I almost always think of Seth in regards to the push or pull marketing strategy. The idea here is that entrepreneurs tend to push their content and information out to those who may be interested in learning more. I have to admit that is tempting, at least when you are just starting out.

But the truth is that you will do much better all around if you are willing to rethink your strategy and switch almost exclusively over to what is referred to as *pull* marketing. This is where you allow prospects, clients, and customers to come to you for what you have to offer instead of pushing it in their faces. Allow me to provide some examples of how this could work in your business.

I create content almost daily, and then syndicate and distribute that content in a number of ways through various channels and platforms. This is an attempt on my part to push out this content, filled with my ideas and knowledge and expertise into the cyberspace inhabited and frequented by my prospects. Many times this is successful and brings new people into my world. If I had not been aggressive and determined in the way I achieve this goal each day these new people may have never discovered me and how I may serve them in becoming more successful as an online entrepreneur. Or so I think...

Pull marketing in my business consists of going about my daily routine and allowing the people who find me to decide whether they will connect with and follow me or not. If you found this book by searching for information on any of a variety of the topics included within these pages, or read a review of this book or of one of my previous ones, or heard about it on a podcast or an interview then you came to me as a result of pull marketing. You pulled me into your sphere and realm of consciousness because you were attracted to or resonated with something I stand for and shared.

Whereas push marketing seems to make sense for those just getting started as an entrepreneur, allowing the concept of pull marketing to unfold naturally will be far more effective over time. Patience can be a virtue in business, even though the waiting may be maddening to endure at first.

The idea of maintaining a strong work ethic comes into play when you are ready to see your business in a new light. Trust the process and know that what you offer others is desirable and helpful to what they are working to achieve.

Part III Action Steps

Think back to that time in your life when you honestly knew and believed that anything was possible. What did that look like, feel like, taste like all those years ago? Remember as much detail as you can about those days when no one and no situation could deter you from your dreams. Write about this in the journal or notebook you are keeping as you go through this book.

When you think about making major changes in your life, how does this make you feel? Write down one or two of your experiences with change throughout your life. Did everything work out the way you had hoped for, or was it even better than you had imagined?

Do you ask others for help when contemplating a new situation? What has that experience been like for you over the years? Think about and write down your process for asking others for help.

Are you a courageous person? Think about this question and answer it in the journal you are keeping for this book. What does the quote from Anais Nin mean to you and how does it make you feel?

"Life shrinks or expands in proportion to one's courage."

Think about how your life will be different as a result of rethinking and then taking positive actions regarding your work ethic. Can you see that anything is possible once you are willing to level up in this way? Write about the possibilities and imagine your wildest dreams becoming a reality as a result of changing your thinking, taking action, shifting your attitude, and thus altering your behavior over time to give you a new outlook on life and results that are meaningful to you.

What are your thoughts around the concept of transactional versus relational interactions with others? When you go into a retail establishment is it more transactional, or have they made the shift to creating a relational experience for you? Pay attention to this difference and write down what occurs for you.

Is there a way for you to turn a transactional experience and relationship into a relational one, perhaps by engaging someone in conversation and asking them their name to begin with and then moving on from there?

Part IV – How to Get Started

We didn't have a lot when I was growing up, and it's the best thing that happened. I appreciate everything. I developed a strong work ethic, and I don't take anything for granted.
~ Sarah-Jessica Parker

After reading all of this you may be thinking that you're ready to jump in to rethinking your work ethic, but don't know how and where to begin. If that's the case, congratulations on being ready to take action. And of course, I would not dream of leaving you high and dry after bringing you so far. This is what you may fondly look back upon at some point in your future as being the "good part" of this book.

This section is where I will give you more of a step by step blueprint on how to begin. And even though I will preface this section and that statement by saying there is never a true blueprint or step by step procedure for entrepreneurship, there is certainly one for changing your work ethic in the way I am describing and recommending within these pages. Once again I will share a story with you in order to get this discussion off the ground properly.

A few years ago I met a man who would be instrumental in how I perceived my life and business from a global perspective and standpoint. Early on he commented that I had a stronger work ethic than that of anyone he had previously observed among the people he encountered and interacted with regularly. I took that as a great compliment. Here was someone who had been working on six continents for almost three decades, consulting with some of the most powerful people and innovative companies in the world in the areas of economics, politics, law, and new media technology, and he had noticed my work ethic. Yes, that made my day.

He and I continue to work together on various aspects of my business, including the way I reach out to people I don't know already who are located in remote corners of the world. This has resulted in some friendships and business ventures I would never have thought possible.

And even earlier in my entrepreneurial career people began to notice and comment on my time management strategies and productivity skills, leading me to write *Time Management Strategies for Entrepreneurs: How to Manage Your Time to Increase Your Bottom Line* with the late Geoff Hoff back in 2012.

All of this experience comes into focus as I guide you through the steps, activities, and exercises that will stretch you far out of your comfort zone and into a world where anything is possible and most likely probable, if you are willing to commit to doing the work. It is in this section where you will begin to put into use what I have already shared and to begin your own process of not only rethinking but also of changing your work ethic, embracing the struggle, and exceeding your own potential in your life and business with the help of my proven strategies.

The Steps

Allow your mind to take you into the future for the next few minutes. Imagine what it will be like when you have a new outlook on life based on your perception of the work ethic. What does it feel like to know that you can have, do, and be anything you want? Is it empowering? Does it make you feel giddy? Or does life suddenly seem easier and more fair? As the now famous quote above from "Star Wars Episode V: The Empire Strikes Back" states, we must do or do not. There is no try. Let's explore some ways you can get started right now.

The Tribal Perspective

I have long been a student of thinking about life from a tribal standpoint. Perhaps it's due to being an only child, but once I was exposed to this concept of being a part of a tribe it became a way of thinking that has served me well over this past decade or so.

My first tribal experience came in 2005 when I attended a four day camp for business owners and entrepreneurs. It was just the beginning of my entrepreneurial journey and I had no idea what I was in for that weekend. Being out in the wilderness with people you have never met has a way of getting to the core of your belief system and foundation for maneuvering through your life in a way that exposes you as a raw and vulnerable human being.

Our leaders explained that a tribe was a place where you belonged, and that everyone had value and worth to the group. And similar to a family, no one is left behind in a tribe, no matter what. We were then given clear goals to focus upon, something that is common to all great performances and accomplishments throughout our lifetimes.

Next we were taught the difference between competence and commitment. Competence is related to one's knowledge and transferable skills from previous life and work experiences. This is entirely skill based.

Commitment is attitude based. This is one's motivation and confidence in their ability to complete a task. You can make up for your lack of skills and knowledge by making a greater commitment to a project or goal.

When you combine competence with commitment you have individuals and groups that are capable of climbing mountains and achieving goals that have seemed humanly impossible in the past.

That four day experience over a decade ago served as the prelude to what was to come on my entrepreneurial journey, one that continues to take me into unchartered territory and to new heights of performance and accomplishment.

Where Will You Find Your Tribe?

I found my tribe at the first live event I attended. Already having been working online for almost two years, it was at Big Seminar in Atlanta during the spring of 2008 where everything came together for me. A thought leader and brilliant marketer named Armand Morin had already been hosting his Big Seminar events for several years when I finally made the decision to see what it was all about.

There were almost two thousand people attending that spring and I only knew two of them before I arrived at the conference center. And I hadn't met either of them in person until the first day of the event. Armand provided lavish buffets for lunch and dinner as a part of his events and this gave everyone time to catch up with friends and to make some new ones.

As an introvert and a new entrepreneur this situation was overwhelming to me. I did manage to connect with the two people I knew and to also make some new friends. Over those next three days I settled into a routine of connecting with people I did not know and finding out more about them. This was helpful on many levels. It turned out I was not the only person who was relatively new to online marketing and live events. And the people who were seasoned and well connected were more than happy to connect with me and to introduce me to people they had known and collaborated with for a longer period of time. To this day I continue to be friends and colleagues with about a dozen entrepreneurs I met at Big Seminar that weekend in Atlanta.

As I continued my entrepreneurial journey that year and learned that business consisted of what is referred to as "learnable skills", I knew that if I was simply willing to continue learning and to make a full commitment to what I wanted to achieve in my new business there was an excellent chance that I would not only succeed, but excel in my efforts. This was the beginning of rethinking my own work ethic and changing my life. It was as though I had discovered a super power that others had access to but most chose to ignore.

It was through this group that I entered, competed in, and won the top prize of twenty-five thousand dollars cash just a year later in the "Better Your Best" contest hosted annually by Armand Morin and his team at Big Seminar. I was virtually unstoppable as I grew my business over a one year period and changed everything I was doing. My focus, clarity, and discipline had never been so strong within me and I was unbeatable in this competition.

I made it my goal to hold myself accountable and to remind myself daily of just what was possible within my life. And almost immediately after embracing this new mindset everything started to turn around for me, including my health, personal relationships, and my new business.

And as far as accountability goes, I see this as almost the exact opposite of something you might recognize as entitlement. I'll discuss my thoughts and feelings around this concept more fully before the end of this book.

And a side note here; after winning the Better Your Best Contest in November of 2009 I went on to mentor three more people for this contest, two of whom took first place and one taking second place in this fierce competition. It just goes to show that by surrounding yourself with the people who are exhibiting a strong work ethic and embracing the struggle, anyone can exceed their own potential.

The Building Blocks of Work Ethic

Here are ten traits and characteristics that I have identified as being crucial to rethinking and expanding your work ethic. It is my belief and experience that any one of us has the wherewithal to develop or build upon who we already are to better embody all of these:

- Uncompromised Integrity
- Respectfulness
- Sense of Responsibility
- A Focus on Quality and Workmanship
- Dependability
- Discipline
- Dedication
- Determination and Perseverance
- Accountability
- Humility

Now let's go into greater detail about each of these concepts and how they relate to rethinking the work ethic...

Uncompromised Integrity - I am defining integrity to refer to something much larger and more important than honesty. Integrity is at the core of your very being. One who lives in integrity doesn't even need to think about whether or not something is honest or dishonest. There is no gray area when it comes to integrity; it's either right or wrong and must be intuitive. Perhaps integrity can best be explained as referring to what someone says or does when no one else is looking.

Respectfulness - We begin to learn respect for others and ourselves at a very young age from parents, teachers, and others in our lives. Respect is a two part process. First, it's about putting others first in regards to their wants and needs. When you listen to someone else, really hear them, and then think, speak, and act with their best interest at heart you are exhibiting the kind of respect I am referring to here. Secondly, it's about respecting yourself and always believing that you are worthy of and deserve respect from others. It's not alright for anyone to treat you poorly or for you to have to excuse someone's bad behavior towards you for any reason.

Sense of Responsibility – Some people are more responsible than others are by choice. And there are other people who seem to repel the notion of taking responsibility and almost revel in their willingness to allow others to shoulder their share of responsibility. Over the past decade I have gone to the far end of the spectrum by taking responsibility for everything that crosses my life's path. Whether it was Hurricane Andrew in 1992 that took all of my worldly possessions within a few hours in the middle of the night, or being diagnosed with breast cancer at the age of thirty-seven without having made poor choices or engaged in high risk behavior, I gladly assume all responsibility.

More joyous occurrences continue to come into my life each day than unhappy events, and I take full responsibility for them as well. This sense of responsibility frees you up to allow both positive and negative experiences to come into your life experience, further empowering you to enjoy your journey along the way.

A Focus on Quality and Workmanship – There is nothing like the experience of observing something that exemplifies fine quality and superior workmanship. When I was in the first grade we had carpentry (we weren't actually using saws or anything dangerous here) as an after school activity. I chose to make a small wooden car to give to my neighbor, a little boy who wasn't yet old enough to attend school all day and whom longed to be a part of it all. I must have sanded those two wooden blocks for what seemed like weeks before the teacher nodded his approval. Then the painting was next, and that's where I became tired of the process and wanted to cut corners. But the teacher got me back on track and I brushed the shiny red paint in long, broad strokes to match the grain of the wood. By the time I added the axles and the wheels I had created a product I was quite proud of completing and then presenting to my little friend.

This concept translates into business when you create a product or a training program that others benefit from. I'm not talking about seeking perfection here at all. What you want to focus on is creating a high quality end product that exemplifies the workmanship you are capable of and wish to be known for as an entrepreneur.

Dependability - This can be defined as doing what you said you would do, no matter what it takes to make that happen. Whether you have agreed to meet a friend for lunch, borrowed money from someone kind enough to lend it to you, or promised yourself that you would complete a project by a certain date and in a certain way, if you are dependable you will do what needs to be done and not make any excuses. If you have ever had an experience with someone who is not dependable, then you know how they lose credibility in your eyes the very first time they let you down. Strive to be the picture of dependability in everything you undertake.

Discipline - This was not a concept I embraced until starting my online business. Prior to that I was someone who regularly changed my mind, often did not finish what I started, and used phrases and terms like "I don't feel like it" frequently when it came to achieving my goals. During the first month of leaving my teaching job and real estate clients behind I attempted to start and run my online business with this same attitude. That did not work at all and it was at that point in time when I realized that I was going to have to discipline myself if I was to have any chance at all at success. And to my surprise and delight it turned out that I craved discipline and thrived in that climate. The rest, as they say, is history.

Dedication - Being dedicated to what you are doing in your life and business makes all of the difference. Early on I decided to think of what I was doing as having a Mission Statement and that helped me to internalize my dedication. It makes my dreams and goals bigger than myself and gives me a vision of what I want to achieve. I often describe what I do within my online business as "dedicating my life to helping others become successful entrepreneurs."

Determination and Perseverance - My thinking for the past decade has always included the idea of never, ever giving up. No matter how difficult or challenging something is, I continue to be determined to persevere until whatever it is has been completed. This forces me to think outside the box, to ask others for help on a regular basis, to dig deep for solutions, and to not complain about the struggle. This also allows me to take credit for the outcome and to feel extremely proud of myself each time I have reached a goal. This doesn't mean you won't alter your strategy with something you are working on. Instead, course correct and keep moving until you have reached your goal.

Accountability - Ultimately, you must be accountable to yourself every day to achieve your goals and complete your tasks. During this decade I have been working as an online entrepreneur there has been a resurgence of having an "accountability partner" and much talk about staying accountable to others. Even though this may be helpful for you at some point as you rethink your work ethic, look inward and do the things you know are important so that you can feel accountable to yourself. if you have ever gone on a diet or agreed to do something equally as challenging for someone else, you know that being accountable to another person is a recipe for excuses and failure. Don't go down that path.

The flip side of accountability is entitlement, which I describe as the belief that you have the right to something and are deserving of special treatment and privileges. Instead, I strongly believe that each of us must earn what we receive and can best accomplish this by staying in integrity and being accountable to ourselves and to our Mission.

Humility - There is a song by country artist Tim McGraw called "Humble and Kind" that explains in part how to live humbly around others. My favorite line is "don't steal, don't cheat, and don't lie" because it is simple, obvious, and so true. Growing up my mother had used a saying that was something about not having to tell people how good you are because the cream always rises to the top. This was meant to keep me from being a braggart and talking about myself so much. But those years of being reminded of this did not keep me from boasting about anything material I had obtained or achievements I had reached. It wasn't until much later when I learned by observing others why being humble was such a virtue and is indeed a worthy goal.

Before we get to the Action Steps for this section of the book, make a list of these traits and characteristics, add any others you can think of that I did not include here, and begin to write down your thoughts and experiences around them. This will serve you well as we move through the remainder of what I am sharing with you here.

Putting Yourself First

Just as we are instructed in an airplane to affix our own oxygen mask first before assisting another passenger, even if it's a young child, we must put ourselves first if we are to ever be there for others. This may sound selfish, but upon further examination we see that this is best for all concerned.

I've been a Rotarian since 2006 (Rotary is an international service organization whose priority projects include bringing clean water to people in countries where this is a daily issue and eradicating polio from our planet) and we have something called "The 4-Way Test" that goes like this:

1. Is it the TRUTH?
2. Is it FAIR to all Concerned?
3. Will it build GOODWILL and BETTER FRIENDSHIPS?
4. Will it be BENEFICIAL to all concerned?

This test is profound in its simplicity, and was created during the Great Depression by Rotarian Herbert J. Taylor when he was attempting to save a company from bankruptcy by closely adhering to strong moral and ethical principles.

The goals continue to be ones I strive for and where I have learned that putting myself first is the logical first step to doing things that will be truthful, fair, and beneficial for others. I hope you will consider this 4-Way Test when you put yourself first in order to better serve yourself and others.

Doing It

No one learns to ride a bike from a book, or even a video.
You learn by doing it.
Actually, by not *doing it. You learn by doing it wrong, by falling off, by*
getting back on, by doing it again.
~ Seth Godin

I can always tell when someone I am mentoring is actually taking action. How can I tell? They have different questions. Like the quote at the beginning of this chapter states so clearly, you learn by *doing*. Whether you are doing it right or doing it wrong at the beginning, or even once you are a seasoned entrepreneur or business owner is not important. You must do something every day to move you closer to your goals. Because if you are not moving closer to your goals you are moving further away from them. Every action we take every single day can be categorized in this way in regards to some aspect of our lives.

Knowing what to do is where a mentor can come in handy and be a valuable resource to save you time and money on your journey. I will make my best effort to mentor you here, even though you and I will be at somewhat of a disadvantage because we cannot interact directly. Instead, I will share my best suggestions, recommendations, and advice and it will be up to you to read, think, implement, and then seek out someone to work closely with when the time is right for you.

And my last comment on mentorship is that you must ask any potential mentor if they are currently working with a mentor. The answer must be a resounding Yes!, or that person has reached a point where they no longer believe they need or will benefit from having a mentor. That's a dangerous point for any of us to reach and actually that point does not exist. Enough said.

Just this morning a man on my email list wrote to me asking about one of my products. I wrote back and answered his question but also asked where his main site was so that I could take a look. Like more than ninety-five percent of the people "trying" to start an online business he wrote that he was stuck in "the paralysis of analysis" mode. He added that there's so much to learn and he doesn't really want to make newbie mistakes that may significantly hurt him in the future in terms of his reputation, forcing him to have to start all over from the beginning at some later point in time.

I answered him back saying that the only mistake he could make would be in not starting. I added that I have over three hundred sites and about sixty products and they are all works in progress. And then I wrote that when the pain of having spent so much time and money is greater than the fear of making mistakes, which is most certainly a guarantee, then he'd be ready to begin.

Go back to Chapter Four on "Do This...Don't Do That" where I discuss all of this in greater detail if you can relate to this man and the feelings he expressed to me within his email. Take some time to write down in your journal or notebook what jumps out at you here.

I strongly believe that we are all so much more capable and powerful than we ever quite imagine or believe about ourselves and that it should not take a catastrophe or other monumental situation or set of circumstances to bring these qualities out in ourselves. Look for the daily opportunities to think about, take action, and then behave in a way that will become your new normal. Remember that our thoughts, actions, beliefs, and behaviors lead to us changing our nature. I have this written down and carry it with me everywhere I go. My goal is to change my nature one thought, one belief, and one action at a time.

Tactics versus Strategies

When you are just getting started with anything new in your life or business it's the tactics that must be tackled first. Think back to when you were learning to drive a car, as an example. You had to do everything in slow motion in order to know the steps and remember them. Just starting the car and placing your foot on the correct pedal was something you had to think about.

My newest car has a push button ignition, so once again I had to learn the tactics of starting the car before I could move ahead any further.

Everything in life can be thought of in this way. Enjoy the journey of learning the tactics because once you make the transition into learning and applying the strategies everything begins to flow.

As I write this fifteenth book I am reminded of the time it took me to go from being a tactical writer to a strategic one. It seemed like forever for me to think of the next idea I would write about, create a notes document in which to record my thoughts and ideas, and finally begin an outline that would allow my book to take shape.

Over time I was able to hasten this process to where my outline would come together in days instead of weeks. I have already described what it is like these days to have my books almost write themselves as I flesh out the thoughts and ideas I originally wrote down in my notes. You can reach this level as well, as long as you are actually "doing" the thing you want to accomplish in its initial stages so that it can come to fruition.

Daily Tasks

So you may be wondering what I recommend you do each day in order to be a successful entrepreneur. I will share my daily tasks and include my recommendations for you in great detail within the next chapter, and depending upon where you are in the process you will begin to make changes in your own daily routine of activities. If you are rethinking your work ethic, more than willing to embrace the struggle, and ready to exceed your highest potential then you will be able to master anything we discuss here in record time and in a joyous manner.

The most important tasks you will engage in every day as an entrepreneur are writing and creating. After that comes teaching and mentoring. It's interesting to me that after half a century of thinking of myself as a logical, left-brained individual I have now come to think of myself as and make a living from creative processes almost exclusively.

In the next chapter we are going to take a look at what it will be like once you take action on what you have been learning here. I call this "A day in the life..."

A Day in the Life...

There will be obstacles.
There will be doubters.
There will be mistakes.
But with hard work, there are no limits.
~ Michael Phelps

I can remember the exact day when I woke up a changed person. It was a cool, crisp April morning in 2005 and I had awakened around four, a full hour earlier than my usual time. As I took care of my pets, prepared a light breakfast, showered and got ready for my day I knew that something about me was different. It was a knowing that I could do what needed to be done that day in a way that would serve others while still valuing and honoring who I was and what I needed from my life.

It was a weird feeling because it was completely foreign to me, but I went with it because it felt empowering and enlightening. It was the feeling of total and complete confidence in myself as a human being, something that was rare for me at that point in my life experience.

Now It's Your Turn

For one day I want you to experience what it is like to have a stronger work ethic than you ever imagined. This involves embracing any struggles you encounter and knowing that you will be exceeding your highest potential every step of the way.

So, how do you begin this one day experience and journey? It all begins with your attitude.

On the day I described above, I woke up with a positive attitude.

Believing that everything will unfold as it is meant to manifest is an amazing way to live your life. So I want you to do the same, starting with this one day.

If you are new to this type of thinking about your life, taking action on your thoughts, and behaving in a way that will support your thoughts and actions you will want to choose a day that is less stressful than what you might be used to most every day. Choose a day off from work, or a day where you are not expected to do more than you typically do on any given day. I want you to experience a dramatic shift in your life and being under pressure does not help when you are making positive efforts towards changing your life. My clients have reported having the best experiences when they are spending the day with family and friends or volunteering for a worthy cause.

Make sure you have had a good night's sleep and a light breakfast to prepare you for your day. And take at least a few minutes to stretch and then meditate on what you are about to experience. Leave your house in enough time to arrive a little early to your destination. I always have something to read, a notebook to write in, and my smart phone to check emails in my possession at all times, so I am never impatient at having to wait and am never late for an appointment. This strategy alone has saved me so much stress over the years I cannot even begin to explain what it has meant to my sanity and well being.

And as you are driving or walking to your destination today, take it a little more slowly than usual. It isn't a race and you've left home a little earlier than you would have, so enjoy the trip and look for things you may not have noticed in the past. I have found that if I walk or drive at about three quarters of the speed that is usual for me I see things that I was sure weren't there before. Actually it was all there to begin with, but I was always dashing by and did not notice.

Before you get out of your car set your intention for the day, or at least for this first segment of the day. Who will you be spending time with? What will you be doing? How can you serve the people and the situation in a way that will honor and value both you and them? I'll bet you have not ever thought about your day in this way before. Am I correct?

When you first encounter the people you will be spending time with today, try to feel out their mood. See if you can be helpful with anything they need, and offer to do something extra to lighten their load. This can be as simple as holding the door open for them, carrying a bag or a box, or just listening to what they have to say. Most people are still caught up with emotions and drama from the day before and need to get that out of their system before they can fully be present for today. You will begin to observe this trait in others and wonder why you ever allowed other people's issues to cloud your own thinking and actions in a way that kept you from moving ahead with your own dreams and goals every waking moment.

Once you have served the others, take a few minutes to get back into your head and reset your intention for the day, if necessary. Be aware that you will always be in full control of your emotions and that your thoughts, actions, beliefs, and behavior will reflect that to the outside world. Resist the urge to share every personal detail of your life with everyone, and reserve that instead for the one or two people who are closest to you. This will make a huge difference in how confident you are and how you are perceived by others in the long run.

As you interact with the others throughout your day, remember to be a good listener. Over the years I have practiced saying as little as possible about myself while also asking others about themselves so they could share. This has been a good lesson to me on an ongoing basis as to how best to serve those around me. Listening to others is a gift they will appreciate greatly and always remember when they think back to their time with you.

Now you are engaged in the tasks and activities you set out to do today. This is the work and this is where I want you to step up your work ethic to a level that is at least slightly uncomfortable for you. Yes, I want you out of your comfort zone because this is where the growth occurs. Work hard!

Whatever you are used to doing, do more. However you approached issues in the past, do it differently. And when you're ready to take a breather from all you've done, keep working. This is what it takes to have and maintain a strong work ethic.

Next comes the turning and tipping point. This is where

something happens that used to set you back. Someone says something, there is a mistake or an issue. There are obstacles that seem too steep to overcome, at least for the moment. And now is where your best intentions for the day are held high for all to see. It's a struggle that must be embraced if you are to push forward in your life. How will you handle it?

As the quote at the beginning of this chapter states, *with hard work there are no limits*. That's right. You will work harder than before to figure it out and push through this challenge. This requires you to think on your feet, be bold, and be willing to go above and beyond what you have done in prior situations.

And above all else, do this work joyfully. There is to be no complaining or blaming or wishing this set of circumstances had not occurred. No, you are welcoming this opportunity to embrace yet another struggle to push through it and rise above it. It's all about the struggle at this moment.

And when the crisis has passed you will feel proud of what you were able to accomplish. Instead of thinking, acting, and behaving as you once did you stepped up to the plate and did what was necessary to solve the problem and complete the task. Others see what you did and are amazed at how you handled it. You have taken the next step in this process which is to ultimately change your nature.

Sometimes catastrophe puts us in this space and we almost always rise to the occasion to do what needs to be done. We often hear about someone who went above and beyond when called to do so because someone's life was in danger or some other emergency situation. But what I am suggesting is that you do not wait for a set of circumstances to present themselves before acting in this way. Level up your thinking so that you are ready to step in and take charge of your actions in a way you are not yet used to every single day. This will take some getting used to, and once you have begun to master these beliefs and actions there will be no stopping you.

How does it feel to be you right now? Awesome, I hope.

The Women's Conference

Recently I was invited to a women's conference at a friend's church. I had no idea what to expect and wanted to have this experience. I even invited a friend to join me, and early on that Saturday morning I picked her up so that we could drive to the church together.

My friend did not ask what time this conference would begin, so it wasn't until I arrived at her home that she asked me. That's when I told her that we were early and would time to drive to the church in a leisurely manner, giving us the time to talk and to set our intentions for the day.

Fortunately, I only spend time with open-minded people these days and my friend was excited at the prospects and experiences that awaited us. Our intention for the day and the conference was to connect with people we already knew and to make some new friends, as well as to learn some new things and to open to understanding ideas and concepts we were not yet familiar with in our own lives. We also wanted to be helpful to others.

The struggle I needed to embrace on this day was the idea of spending many hours with so many people. Unlike my friend, who describes herself as "loving people" I am an extreme introvert who needs downtime throughout the day to refresh and regroup after being exposed to many people. I knew this was not possible in this situation so I embraced the struggle and moved forward with a positive and hopeful outlook and perspective.

When we arrived there were women hurrying in with bags and boxes and food items and my friend and I offered to help. This was graciously accepted and so began our day. As we helped to set up the auditorium where the conference was to be held and the kitchen where lunch was to be provided we did a little extra, perhaps something more than we would have done previously. This felt good and the work was completed more quickly than anyone thought possible.

The opening activity was a craft, something I have never excelled in. But I approached it with an open mind and jumped in to learn what to do. It was a part of something called "Operation Gratitude" for those serving in the United States Armed Forces and deployed overseas and we were going to put together paracord "survival" bracelets.

These bracelets are intended to be used in case of emergency by service members. They consist of seven and a half feet of cord and are twisted and tied in a specific way so that the service person can unravel them quickly if they need the cord for any of a variety of reasons. They have a breaking strength of five hundred fifty pounds! The uses include setting up a tent, fishing line, making a tourniquet or a splint, securing a boat to a tree or a tarp between trees, hanging food in trees securely, creating a trip wire, tying objects together for transport, and so many more.

So I listened intently to the directions being given, and I did it correctly on my first try. I was thrilled by this and went on to teach four other women at my table how to do it as well. Over the next hour our group of almost a hundred women made more than three hundred of these bracelets and it was quite a rewarding experience for everyone.

As the day progressed, I set a new intention for each activity. Knowing that being fully present makes such a difference, I turned off my cell phone and put thoughts of family, business, and activities for later that evening out of my mind completely. It was empowering to be a part of this group and to be getting so much from the events that unfolded.

At lunch I found my friend and we volunteered to bring out some of the food from the kitchen to add to the buffet line. Our help was appreciated and lunch moved more quickly than had been anticipated. We sat at a table where two of the women were in wheelchairs and my friend went through the buffet line for them while I made sure they had what they needed at our table. Sometimes it's the smallest acts of kindness that mean the most in the long run. I even have a photograph of my friend serving desserts to everyone at our table while I and another woman began clearing the plates and glasses as part of the cleanup efforts so we could begin the next phase of the conference.

The afternoon speakers, presentations, and activities were also of great interest and I began to think of how I could share some of the ideas with other groups I am involved in. And at the end of the day my friend and I stayed to help clean up. There had been almost a hundred women at the conference and there was much work to do when it was finally over.

As we walked out to the car, my friend shared that this had been much more work than she had expected, but also more rewarding and satisfying than she could have ever imagined. We had made new friends, connected with people we already knew, learned new things, opened up our minds to some unfamiliar ideas and concepts, and been helpful to others. Yes, we had met all of our intentions and then some. And instead of driving home and crashing in front of the television, we decided to attend a charity fundraiser later that evening.

Employing a strong work ethic can be invigorating, even when there is hard work involved. And having this opportunity to spend time with these strong women was awesome.

Applying These Concepts to Business

You may be thinking that it is all well and good to bring joy to others at a social activity, but that it would be quite different in business.

Not really.

The goal is to approach your business in a positive, uplifting, and enthusiastic way each day. I like to begin my day by reaching out to someone I haven't been in contact with for some time. This would be someone who is also working online as an author, entrepreneur, or in some other related capacity. The idea here is to initiate contact to see what we are both working on that might be a good fit for collaboration, affiliation, or just general interest.

For example, this morning I reached out to Justin Popovic, someone I met several years ago when we were both speaking at the same marketing conference. Justin is an expert in motivation and leadership and an accomplished author and online entrepreneur. And his work ethic is awesome in that he left the corporate world to start his online business while married with two young sons.

He had sent me some content to use as I saw fit around the topic of standing out with your business, your brand, and your personality. I saw this as being perfect to repurpose into a short report to add as a bonus for my *Become a Local Celebrity* online training course.

By reaching out to Justin I am able to catch up with what he is working on, to share my recent accomplishments, and to see where we might have some overlap. Then I can ask him how I may serve him and be a blessing in his life and business, at least for today. This leads to a deeper connection and stronger friendship for the coming years.

Throughout my workday I take short breaks to serve those who are a part of my online community. Sometimes they need resources or ideas, while at other times they want direction and encouragement. And they are there to serve me as well, which makes the circle of service complete.

Implement the ideas I am setting forth in this chapter and your life is sure to change in a positive and surprisingly joyous manner.

Social Media Distraction

Distracted from distraction by distraction.
~ T.S. Eliot

First of all I need to preface this chapter by saying that I love social media. I love that it has made our world smaller and more connected. I love that we have a front row seat to some of the most awesome and some of the most revealing moments in history. I love the marketing possibilities it offers. And I love that I have a voice that can be heard equally as loud and as often as that of some of the most brilliant thought leaders in the world.

And that's where my love affair with social media ends. In many ways I feel like a parent who is at first caught up in the excitement of something their child will be able to do, only to find out it will be harmful for the child if you allow it into your life. Climbing trees and skateboarding come to mind here.

I have lost too many potentially excellent entrepreneurs in my mentor program to social media. The distraction element is a huge issue, and the need to find out what others are doing at every moment, as close to "real time" as possible leads to neurotic behavior and an addiction that is not easily overcome.

Lest you think I am being too dramatic with my descriptions here I will share some Case Studies with you so you can perhaps understand this from my perspective.

I worked with someone I will call "Helene" for several years. Helene lived in a small Midwest town and cared for her mother during the day and her toddler grandson several evenings a week while her daughter was at work. She wanted to start an online business to bring in some income to help her family and I was thrilled to take her on as a client.

Helene was blogging regularly, creating products and courses around the topics of blogging and technology, and sharing her life and business on social media when she had the time in her busy schedule.

Over the course of a few months I saw that Helene was spending much less time working in her business and more and more time on Facebook, Instagram, and Twitter. During our mentoring calls she explained to me that she was using social media to connect with new prospects and build relationships with established marketers. This seemed to be in line with what I was teaching and I encouraged her to continue, but also to not lose focus on creating content and new products.

The following month we had a call and I warned her against spending too much time on social media to the exclusion of time creating content, information products, and courses. She wasn't attending our group mentee calls and webinars and didn't answer my emails for several days sometimes.

Another month passed and Helene dropped out of my program altogether. She was just starting to see some success in her business and wanted to go it alone for awhile. Every week I would check to see what she and my other current mentees were doing on Facebook and I was shocked at what I found.

Helene was now spending hours each day engaged in discussions on a variety of topics, none of which included her business. In fact, there was no longer any discussion around her business and someone who did not know her would not even know she had a business.

And the promotions of products from sites like the Warrior Forum, ClickBank, and JV Zoo covered her personal page. These tended to be ten dollar or even less offerings around internet marketing topics which had little or nothing to do with what she was building in her own business. Just to be clear, I use these low cost sites and recommend the people and products there regularly, but the idea of slapping an offer from them on to your social media pages is useless and degrades and dilutes what you are working to achieve as an online entrepreneur.

After two weeks of seeing this I stopped visiting her page altogether. I was no longer working with her, so I had become a voyeur who had no business checking up on her. The last I heard Helene had taken a job in a city more than an hour from her home on order to earn some income for her family. This broke my heart and there was nothing at all I could do to alleviate the situation.

When people in my daily, offline life tell me they are too distracted to complete a project I can predict they will tell me it is social media making this so. My advice is always the same - turn it off! I cannot imagine accomplishing my goals with the cyber noise of the world buzzing in the background. And I certainly do not need to know what is happening anywhere in the world in real time.

While I was in the classroom I kept my cell phone turned off or on vibrate and in my purse in the closet. One day I forgot to turn it off and it rang during my math lesson. I simply ignored it and went on teaching my lesson. One of the children raised his hand to ask me if I was going to answer it. He said it might be an emergency. This is what I had to say to that:

"What kind of emergency might it be? You mean like my house is burning down or someone has to be taken to the hospital? In either case, there are others to be called long before me. And if I am truly needed everyone knows that I am right here at the moment. I'm sure someone would call the school's office and they would call us through the speaker system or send someone to our classroom to tell me to come to the office immediately."

The children nodded in agreement and we went on with our lesson. I told them that teaching them was the most important thing in the world to me at that moment and they smiled because they knew I meant that sincerely. After lunch I informed them that the call had been from my dentist, reminding me of my appointment after school the following day. They were satisfied in knowing these details.

Here is yet another Case Study around this topic of distraction:

"Todd" was going through a difficult divorce. I knew that because he began to share many of the details on social media. I was saddened at first, and then embarrassed to watch this all unfold. he was clearly going through one of the hardest and most painful times of his life and Todd chose to reach out to people he barely knew instead of maintaining a more private persona during this time.

I had watched Todd's business grow over the previous five years and respected his work immensely. Then he began to post multiple times each day with these snippets of his life related to a marriage that had gone sour during the past year or so. He shared some of the most intimate stories you could imagine. Many people commented, sharing their thoughts and opinions on events none of us should have ever known about. Todd was going through a raw and emotional time in his life. It would have been much better, in my opinion, if he had kept all of this more private and definitely not shared it on social media sites where his business connections were apt to read about it.

Finally I unfriended and unfollowed Todd on social media, and not long after I unsubscribed from his mailing list because I no longer thought of him in the same way. After evaluating the situation this seemed to make the most sense.

Are you spending some of your most valuable hours each day on the various social media sites? In all of these years I have kept my social media engagement down to fifteen minutes a day total, and on many days I do not even visit any of the sites. Yet my business flourishes as a result of sharing my content and interacting with others in this way. It can be done without affecting the other areas of your life.

Part IV Action Steps

Life is not an audition. We're actually on stage for all to see as we live our lives day in and day out. Are you still practicing to make it perfect, or are you jumping in each day and skinning your knees as you experience all that your life has to offer? What do you think about when I share this quote from Yoda of Star Wars fame?

"Do...or do not. There is no try."

Are you actively "doing it" when it comes to your life and business? Make a list of your recent successes to see what you are accomplishing, and another list of the things you are putting off and why that is the case with each one. See if you can overcome the reasons you are convincing yourself of for not starting or completing something that you are telling yourself you truly want to achieve.

Let's revisit the traits I have identified as being crucial to success as an entrepreneur with a strong work ethic:

- Uncompromised Integrity
- Respectfulness
- Sense of Responsibility
- A Focus on Quality and Workmanship
- Dependability
- Discipline
- Dedication
- Determination and Perseverance
- Accountability
- Humility

Which ones of these jump out at you? How do you define each of these, based on your own beliefs and values?

What are your thoughts on the tribal perspective I discussed at the beginning of this section? Have you found your tribe? Write about this in your journal or notebook.

Think about the differences between competence and commitment. Remember that competence is skill based, whereas commitment is based on your attitude.

What did you think about after reading the chapter on "A Day in the Life..."? Are you implementing anything I shared there, either in your personal life or in your business? Will you now implement something you see as being valuable?

Has social media become a distraction for you? What will you change about the time you spend on these sites and the manner in which you interact with others?

Part V – What's Next?

Take up one idea. Make that one idea your life – think of it, dream of it, live on that idea. Let the brain, muscles, nerves, every part of your body, be full of that idea,
and just leave every other idea alone.
This is the way to success.
~ Swami Vivekanandahe

If you've arrived at this section after reading and implementing everything I have shared so far, I applaud you. Few get this far by reading and taking action straight through with any of my books, so you have already shown yourself that you are indeed ready for what's next in your life and business.

I like to think of this next step as the "mastery" level. We all wish to master specific concepts and areas of our lives and our businesses and you now have some excellent tools in your toolbox to do just that. As an entrepreneur, and especially as one working online you have the distinct opportunity to reach people all over the planet and to serve them in a way others cannot. You alone hold the power to enrich the lives of so many with what you do.

Also, know that you will have little or no competition once you have leveled up your work ethic. Few people, if any within your circle of influence will be able to maintain the type of stamina, enthusiasm, and daily accomplishment you will be able to exhibit, and most will fall away from the pack as you emerge the frontrunner. This happens all of the time in business, but also in sports, the arts, politics, and academia. You are a winner!

We all want to follow a leader who is willing to share their processes with us. Just as I was drawn to and learned from Mark, the fellow teacher I told you about near the beginning of this book, others will want to connect with you and change their lives over time by adopting a strong work ethic.

And with this great power comes great responsibility, so be willing to accept that as you move forward. Hold your head high, knowing that you have the confidence to be proud of what you are achieving and are ready to help others to do the same.

Doors will open and opportunities present themselves that were hidden and unavailable in your past. As these increase naturally and unfold over time you will understand the true value of living in a global economy. And if you haven't written a book already, know that authorship is imminent.

Now let's move forward together to discuss the role of the process, the specialist, the local celebrity, and the leader in your journey of rethinking your work ethic, embracing the struggle, and exceeding your own potential.

The Process

The successful warrior is the average man,
with laser-like focus.
~ Bruce Lee

There is most definitely a correlation between the time it takes someone to have an idea and the time they implement it. When I was just getting started as an entrepreneur it used to take me months to put my ideas into motion. I made it a goal to speed this process up significantly and these days I will implement something, at least in its initial stage within a day or two. It's due to my laser focused mindset when it comes to my business and what I need to do in order to achieve my goals each day.

How can you speed up your process by utilizing what I have been teaching you here in this book? If you have honestly rethought your existing work ethic, you already have a clear and distinct advantage over those who are still living in some state of mediocrity in comparison.

Let's take the concept of creating a new online course as an example. And I'll share what I did from start to finish with one of my more recent ones, Really Simple Online Courses. In this context, *the process* becomes its own entity in your rethinking of the work ethic.

My Entrepreneurial Process

In December of 2015 I was once again ready to reinvent myself and my business and decided that I would create a series of online courses around the "Really Simple" branding. I had actually created Really Simple Podcasting the previous month and liked how that brand appealed to my target audience. So I sat down and created a list of everything I would teach, including affiliate marketing, information products, content marketing, membership sites, short reports, authority blogging, copywriting, sales strategies, email marketing, list building, and so on. And then the bright light turned on and it came to me that people would want to learn how I was able to create all of these online courses and Really Simple Online Courses was added to my list that day.

Yes, I did all of this is one sitting, took a short break, and then purchased all of the domains I would need to carry this new plan out as soon as possible. There's nothing worse than coming up with a probable winning idea and then finding out at some point that others already own the domain names you were counting on to bring your plan to fruition.

The next step was to take a look at anything I had done previously to see what was similar, what parts I liked, and what didn't work at all. This process of comparing and contrasting gets you closer to your vision each time you create something new, and I highly recommend it for all of your projects. If you haven't yet created something of your own, look at what others have done and see what works best through your eyes and unique perspective.

Once I had done these three things - made a list of courses I would teach over the next year or so, purchased the domain names I would need, and decided exactly how I wanted these sites and courses to be set up online - it was time for the next step.

The next step in this case was to delegate the creation and set up of the sites to someone on my team who could do what I wanted, the way I wanted it done, in a timely manner. You notice I did not say "overnight" or "in a day or two", but "in a timely manner." Even though my goal is always to implement my ideas quickly, I want the process to unfold over weeks and months so that I have the time to make the changes that will inevitably need to be made with any project you undertake.

Once I had delegated this work, which falls into the category of technology and graphic design I was freed up to actually create the courses. Remember that you only do the things you enjoy and are good at in your business. For me these things include writing, creating products and courses, teaching courses virtually and in person, and mentoring other entrepreneurs.

I'm now going to fast forward to Really Simple Online Courses, the eighth one in my series of online courses...

I begin with a word processing document that will become my notes and outline for the course. By the way, this is the exact same process I use when I am ready to write another book each year. Even today, when this book is three quarters of the way complete I will always refer to my notes and outline before proceeding with the writing.

In the notes and outline I begin listing everything I wanted to cover in this online course on teaching online courses. I also include what I will not teach as a part of the course. In this case that included how to sell your online course to sites such as Udemy.

As the notes and outline start to take shape I begin to create my PowerPoint slides in preparation for what I will be presenting to my students. Simultaneously I begin writing the sales copy that will persuade them to join my course based on the benefits they will derive from this training. Over the years I have learned that my products and courses are better in that they are more complete when I write the sales copy *during* the process of product and course creation instead of doing this part of the process *after* the course is completely written.

The words flow as I remember that everything I am creating is a part of a much bigger picture for my life and business. I always return to my Mission when writing the notes for a new product, course, presentation, or live event and that is the idea that anyone can become a successful entrepreneur.

There is a profound peacefulness about being a high achiever and leader in your field. Even if you haven't thought of yourself as a leader up until this time, this is a natural offshoot of rethinking and living a strong work ethic. You will naturally begin to attract other high achievers into your sphere of influence and circle of friends and business associates. This alone is reason enough to make these changes in your life.

As a role model for others in business you set the bar and then raise it to meet the demands of your market. You'll have endless ideas and need to record them all to incorporate them into current projects and for future use.

But I digress. Let's get back to the tactics involved in creating my online course.

My site is set up. My sales copy is written. The slides containing the information I will teach are complete. I have added some bonuses and additional materials to the course. What is left?

Actually this next piece begins while I am still in the process of creating the online course. It's also the most important piece in many respects, as it will dictate how well my course will do once it is released to the world. It's the part where I reach out to others in my field to let them know what I am creating and how it will benefit the people in their community. This part of the process is something I refer to as relationship marketing and this is what separates the average marketer from the high achieving entrepreneur.

I work with about twenty newer online entrepreneurs each year in my Platinum Mastermind group. These people were hand selected and chosen from within my Online Marketing Incubator program because they were ready to play at a higher level, in my opinion. The biggest issue we deal with on a daily basis is relationship marketing. And as much as I extol the value of reaching out to others early on, the more they resist. And I get it. And as a mentor it is my responsibility to break everything down in a way that will be useful for those I am working with, in an individualized manner.

I am an introvert, as are many of the people I work closely with in my programs. I understand those who do not enjoy meeting and interacting with others all day long. Classroom teaching suited me because I was with my students for ninety percent of my workday and that was comfortable for me. The ten percent of the day I spent with the other teachers, parents, and school administrators was not something I naturally looked forward to in my work. So when people come to me and tell me they are not comfortable with reaching out to people they do not yet know I completely understand. I understand and then advise them to "do it anyway."

Just this week I reached out to one of my mentees to find out when she was going to launch her new course. When we spoke on the phone she shared that she had emailed six people several days earlier and had not heard back from even one of them. She said that she was discouraged and for that reason had not contacted any of the others on her list and had not contacted me to discuss what had happened.

Never, ever allow yourself to be discouraged! Instead, step back and take a closer look at what transpired. In this case my client's emails had been overlooked because they were not as personal as they could have been. Within a few minutes we came up with a new strategy to reach the twenty people she had determined would be a good fit for promoting the course she had created and wanted to sell.

Rethinking your work ethic involves getting out of your comfort zone regularly, even on purpose. If this is one of the struggles you must embrace, then do it joyfully. Remaining inside of your protected bubble will not serve you in any way. Stick your finger in that bubble to burst it wide open so you can move on quickly to the next level.

Social media has made some of what I do much easier, but over time that space is saturated with those who are hoping to get in front of the people you need to reach out to so your business will flourish. Be creative and even go "old school" in an attempt to stand out from the crowd. Instead of messaging another thought leader on Facebook, write them a short letter in your own handwriting and mail it to the address at the bottom of their autoresponder emails. And remember that platforms such as Skype are excellent for connecting with people away from the din and cacophony of social media. I compare this to moving away from the ten yard line at a football game and into a private booth at a five star restaurant in order to have a valuable conversation.

Additionally, find a few people you can form friendships with online. I have a few people whom I communicate with almost weekly whom I greatly respect and admire. They are the ones who are willing to take a look at what I am doing and to make intelligent suggestions and offer constructive criticism. This is invaluable to me as a business owner and product creator and I enjoy reciprocating with this as well.

Almost anyone can follow the steps I described at the beginning of this chapter, delegate the parts best completed by others, and offer a product or a service for sale to the world. Almost no one will follow through to the next step in this process by building relationships with those who can make a real difference in their business. If you are the former rather than the latter it's time to review this book and get on board with rethinking your work ethic and embracing the struggle so that you can exceed your highest potential every single day.

Now back to my online course about how to create an online course. Yes, I see the irony here. Anyway, once I have created the course I do not sit around and wait for the day when it will start. No, instead I begin to brainstorm even more ideas on how to add more value to the course before it even begins.

This does not mean that I go back and change and edit and rewrite what I have already created. That's not a good use of my time and would not be beneficial to anyone. I prefer to think outside the box to see what more can be discovered on my journey to providing the best possible training to those who trust me to guide them.

Many times my later ideas will become a bonus training session or a bonus to the overall training course. In my world no ideas or materials are ever wasted when they would be helpful and beneficial to those who trust me to share my knowledge, expertise, and experiences with them.

And something else I'd like to note here is that I always have my next two or three projects on the back burner, waiting until I finish my current one to then hit the ground running with the next. No down time for hard workers with goals to achieve and projects to develop and share!

This is the process I use to create something new in my business on a regular basis. Over time you will come up with your own process. But do not get complacent with what you create, even if it's extremely effective and well received by the marketplace. Be open to rethinking your process and embracing any struggles along the way so that you will continue to exceed your own potential.

The Specialist

People with highly transferable skills may be specialists in certain areas, but they're also incredible generalists, something businesses that want to grow need.
~ Leah Busque

We are living in an age of specialization, and have been for some time. Long gone, at least for the most part are the general practitioners in medicine, law, education, and most other professions. Even the elementary school teacher now specializes in reading, mathematics, social sciences, or the arts and is encouraged to do so by his or her employers. This makes them an even more valuable general education instructor.

You must become a specialist in order to stand out and attract the attention of those in your field. Exceeding your own potential becomes more reasonable and doable when you do so.

Specialists Are Incredible Generalists

As a real estate appraiser I was first asked to be an expert witness in a court case involving a piece of real property back in 1995. The home in question had slid off its foundation and both the property owner and the lender were suing the original appraiser. Because I had experience in building construction (a story mostly irrelevant and much too long to include here) I was called in to give my expert opinion. For this time researching the situation and testifying in the court room I was paid handsomely and it certainly made me think. Something I had additional knowledge about made it able for me to be perceived as an expert and a specialist, thus enhancing my reputation as a generalist in the area of real estate appraisal.

As a classroom teacher I held (and continue to hold) a general education, multiple subject, self-contained classroom, Kindergarten through grade twelve teaching credential in the State of California. Within a few years of teaching I added supplemental credentials with specializations in science and technology to my general education credential. These two supplementals added to my credibility and afforded me opportunities I otherwise would not have had. They also gave me job security when layoffs began within my district a few years later, something I did not expect and could not have predicted earlier on.

I want you to think of your specialization as just that – an enhancement to your expertise in a general area. Just as the dermatologist is a general practitioner first, and later completes additional course work and an internship in this field of specialization, you will be adding to and building upon your knowledge and experience when you choose to specialize.

Let's relate this to your work as a small business owner or an entrepreneur.

Specializing as an Entrepreneur

I began the process of specialization in reverse as an online entrepreneur. My dream was to jump into the internet marketing space immediately, but I did not have the knowledge or experience to do so. After thinking about this during my first couple of months online I decided to find an area where I could specialize and then plan to make a lateral move at some point in the future.

After much contemplation and introspection I decided to specialize in eBooks as a way to get a foothold in my new business. Based on my experiences as a classroom teacher, I concluded that I would have the ability to work with people to plan, research, outline, write, and market their non-fiction eBooks on most any subject they were interested in for their business. I set up my new site at eBook Writing and Marketing Secrets (I still own this domain and now have it forwarded to my main site) and began to build my business.

Now eBook writing and marketing was an extremely specialized area at that time, with only half a dozen people or so actively working in that niche. For me to come along as someone new and attempt to infiltrate this group was quite bold. So the reception I received was more than a little chilly, to say the least.

Lacking confidence at that point in my life, I took a step back before proceeding. Had I taken a misstep with this? Once again I evaluated my qualifications. Over a twenty year period I had taught and edited the writing of students aged five to eighteen, as well as spending two years working at night in adult school with students who also did not speak English as their native language. In addition to this experience I had assisted people working in real estate sales and appraisal with writing out narrative reports and contracts.

When it came to marketing I had almost no experience, but I had decided early on to become a student of marketing and implement what I was learning every single day.

Even though two of the people were not happy, and were quite vocal about it I made the conscious decision to specialize in eBooks for at least the next year before jumping in as a more generalized internet marketer. One year turned into almost two years as I became more efficient and effective with this as a business model.

I then transitioned from being a specialist to becoming a respected generalist, based on my experiences and what I originally wanted to pursue and develop as a part of my online business. And the two people who were upset with me for what they had perceived as "stealing" their niche? They both got over it and we are now colleagues.

Think about this concept at some length to make sure you understand the points I am making and to allow your own beliefs and perceptions around it to flesh out and evolve.

The Local Celebrity

Small business is the backbone of our economy.
Local businesses are a very big deal.
~ Michele Bachmann

A huge part of rethinking your work ethic is about having the confidence to do what you'd really like to do. If your heart is singing around a certain area it's so much easy to go after it when you feel good about yourself and know that you have the support of many others as well.

In 2006 I was a new entrepreneur, having recently left my job as a classroom teacher and winding down my real estate business. I began to attend my local Rotary meeting and was just getting my feet wet when it came to volunteering in the community. It was within this space that I built up my level of confidence and began to excel in my life and business.

I learned quickly that small business owners are very different from employees, as would be expected. What I did not realize at first was that they are responsible for keeping the economy going strong and that they are highly regarded within the communities in which they do business.

During the summer of 2006 I volunteered for several community projects and events. One was at the home of our mayor and was a fundraiser for a local medical clinic. It was set up outside on the gorgeous and sprawling grounds of the mayor's home and volunteers were waiting to park my car when I arrived. Someone asked me if I knew how to mix drinks. I said that I did not, but that I could be an excellent helper. Over the next four hours I fetched ice from the freezer in the garage, brought cases of soft drinks, wine, and liquor in from the shed on a hand cart, and served people a variety of beverages at the makeshift bar that was set up for this purpose. I stayed late and helped clean up, a monumental task after the three hundred guests had departed.

It was what happened between the moment I arrive that night and when the final bag of trash had been hauled to the dumpster that the magic occurred.

Even though I had only lived in this city for a few months and had almost no experience in the volunteer world, that night I made an impact on the people who had attended the charity fundraising event. By working hard and maintaining a friendly and positive attitude I had captured the attention of the movers and shakers in my city. Really I was just being myself, but perhaps more hard working and less likely to show my frustration when things didn't unfold as easily as I had hoped for that night. Like when we ran out of ice and I had to find someone to drive into town to get more, or when I spilled the cart while bringing six more cases of soda back to our work area and had to set it all upright again.

But the evening was a success for this group and I was happy to have been a part of it. Little did I know that the impression I had made on so many people would spill over into my business.

I continued attending Rotary meetings and became a member before the end of that year. This led to more volunteer opportunities of which I looked forward to participating in as often as possible. Because I had been a classroom teacher for twenty years I was drawn to events that included children. And because I had been so poor while growing up I was drawn to events where I could serve those in poverty and the homeless in my city. What's important to not here is that subconsciously I was doing something that proved to be valuable later on; I made an effort to get involved in projects that resonated with who I was as a person.

Along with volunteering locally, here are some other strategies I teach when it comes to becoming a local celebrity in your community:

- Connecting on social media with local people and groups. Use Hashtags (#) to let them know who you are and what you're doing.
- Sending press releases regularly
- Blogging about local people, groups, and events

- Writing a book on your specific topic or a more general one
- Putting together an impromptu speech you can give to local groups
- Fleshing out a full presentation and speech
- Podcasting to interview local leaders
- Writing for local newspapers and magazines
- Producing a show on your local cable television station
- Local radio station shows and interviews
- Partnering with your Chamber of Commerce

Let's go into more detail with each of these. And I will continue to remind you to stay humble at all times for best results.

Volunteering must be done with some thought, if you are going to include this method to become a local celebrity. Choose a group or organization that has a meaningful cause. I'm a former teacher, so it makes sense for me to volunteer for and with groups that have a focus on children. I also grew up in poverty and have a heart for those in need. There are many non-profits and charitable organizations that are involved with projects related to these topics.

Social media makes it possible for you to zero in on the exact people and groups you want to connect with locally. And if you aren't sure, just do a search for your city name and see what comes up.

Look for hashtags, indicated by the pound sign (#) to find out which ones are used. When I do this for either of my cities, Santa Clarita or Santa Barbara I am always surprised to learn about a new event or group I had not heard of previously.

Press releases are an excellent way for you to get known in your community. I can still remember the first two I sent over ten years ago. One was for a project my local Rotary Club had just completed at the elementary school in my neighborhood. They had donated money towards the purchase of playground equipment and accessories for the students with special needs. I can remember how disappointed the people on this committee had been when the local newspaper and radio station did not write or talk about it. So I sent out a press release and everything changed.

Even though it was three months later the newspaper ran a story and the radio station interviewed two Rotarians to discuss what they had done. And then I blogged about it and wrote about it on a real estate site called Active Rain. Another couple of months passed and Rotary International heard about it from what I had written. They contacted me and ended up doing a story on the project that appeared in the May, 2008 Rotarian magazine. That publication goes out to more than a million Rotarians worldwide.

This is an example of why perseverance is key to success in all areas of life. I now describe this playground project as "the project that lives forever" because of what occurred over the period of time long after it was completed. Because I kept sending out information and details the story went around the world and was the first time since our Club had been established almost fifty years ago that we were mentioned in the Rotarian magazine. And the man who headed up the committee is now a nominee for Man of the Year in our city. Also, keep in mind that this all happened before social media, so these days you have even more outlets with which you can distribute information and photographs.

Blogging about local people and events gives you the control over what you share. Whereas a press release will someday be buried among newer information, your blog posts cans be revived and pushed to the forefront once again. It is an honor to write a post about someone in your community to recognize and share their contributions. It is also more personal, as people reading your blog post will then have access to your website and what you have to offer.

Authorship is the next logical step in this process. My first book consisted of fifty blog posts I had written over the previous three months, along with an introduction and a conclusion. I simply divided my posts into sections and included some detail, less than a page in length about each section. The result was a book I was proud of and the status of now being a published author. You can also repurpose everything you write or speak into a variety of other formats. For example, the material contained within this chapter has already been repurposed into blog posts, a short report, and an online course called *Becoming a Local Celebrity*. We all enjoy learning in multiple ways and more than once for maximum and optimal results and this is one way to do that.

When you put together an impromptu speech you are ready to address a group on a moment's notice. For this I will recommend that you choose a specific topic with the general topic of leadership. I cover this in more detail in the very next chapter, so for now just think about what leadership means to you and which aspects of it do you resonate with the most.

The next step is to prepare a complete presentation and speech that is more on the topic you wish to be known for in your business. I started by speaking about how to make huge profits from a tiny list, but this did not resonate with the local business leaders. They understood when I explained that a list in my online marketing world is like a customer database in their world, but having to explain my topic was keeping me at a distance from the very people I wanted to connect with in my community.

I switched over to speaking about social media and how it could be used in business and that went over very well. Making this change early on allowed me to be perceived as an expert, and soon I was being invited to speak to larger groups at better known venues within the area. It was there that I made a name for myself in relation to what I was doing in my business each day. My next jump was to speak about local business marketing and that is what I continue to speak about in both of the cities where I reside.

You will want to create two versions of your speech, as well as two slide presentations. One should take you about twenty to thirty minutes to deliver and answer questions, while a longer version will take you an hour or so. Save it on a flash or thumb drive you carry with you at all times, or have it easily accessible through the cloud with something like Dropbox. And you may even want to go as far as having a one or two page handout at your fingertips. Most venues are equipped with a copy machine so you could be ready to deliver your presentation within ten minutes of being asked to do so. This will separate you from almost everyone else who does not prepare in this way.

Several years ago I was speaking at a large marketing conference and we got word that one of the speakers was delayed in the country he had just been visiting and could not arrive in time for our event. When the event promoter asked if anyone was ready to present only one man stepped forward and had what I am describing to you here. That was a huge opportunity for him and I have never forgotten that incident.

Podcasting and teleseminars enable you to interview local leaders and share information about them and what they are currently involved in. Make sure the focus is mostly on them and what they are doing in the community rather than on you. When you introduce yourself at the beginning and end of the interview you will be able to share a little about yourself and your website.

Local newspapers and magazines are struggling to stay afloat with so much competition from the internet, so your goal of writing a regular column is a win-win scenario for you and the editor of the publication you have in mind.

Make sure to read the newspaper and magazines from cover to cover before approaching them to understand clearly what type of content and style they are looking for with the content they publish. Then prepare an article that fits these criteria and print it out to show to the editors of these publications when you meet with them. Yes, building relationships is the key to success in becoming a local celebrity. I currently write for two offline magazines and have written for several others over the years. In all cases I met the editors in person and then approached them about writing for them. Remember that they do need ongoing content submissions and will be happy to use your content if it fits in with what their readers want to know more about and read.

Your local cable access television station is waiting to produce your show. I have a client who is doing this quite successfully in the area of health and nutrition. She has a weekly show and films them in their studio well in advance. The learning curve was a little bit steep, but once she understood what they wanted she jumped in and made it happen. This is boosting her credibility and allowing her to grow her business in a way most people are not willing to take the time and make the effort to do with consistency.

Most cities and towns have a radio station, so check to see which one is closest to you. When I moved from the San Fernando Valley section of Los Angeles, an area of more than one million residents to Santa Clarita, inhabited at that time by only two hundred thousand people I found their local radio station on my drives back and forth to move into my new home. This was where I found out what was happening in real time and it never occurred to me that someday I would actually be a guest on the radio to discuss the non-profits and service organizations I would become involved with over time. More people than you might imagine listen to the radio while driving, and it's an effective way to get known in your community for both your business and volunteer service.

The Chamber of Commerce is typically a powerful entity in every city, so you'll want to find out more about it right away. I actually connected with Rotary before the Chamber, so when I found out that Rotary was a member of the Chamber I started attending the Chamber's events on behalf of Rotary. They typically have several activities and an open house each month. Take it slowly and see if you need to join or not at this time. Usually the cost for any event is slightly higher for non-members and this can be cost effective when you are just exploring who they are and what they have to offer.

These are the components of becoming a local celebrity in your city or town. It's worthwhile in many ways and can be the right way for you to change the way you think of life and your perspective on life's events. Learning how to stand out in a crowd is crucial to leadership and success for people with a strong and determined work ethic who are working towards worthwhile, achievable goals.

The Leader

If your actions inspire others to dream more, learn more, do more, and become more, you are a leader.
~ John Quincy Adams

Much has been written on the topic of leadership. But how do you become a leader?

I was first exposed to formal training in the area of leadership as a classroom teacher. During the spring or summer of the years 1999, 2002, and 2005 I was invited to a leadership conference held annually at the Asilomar Conference Grounds in Pacific Grove, California. This is one of the most beautiful destinations in northern California, located on the Monterrey Peninsula between Pebble Beach and Big Sur.

When I first found out that teachers I knew were attending this conference it was my assumption that they met some qualifications that I did not in order to be invited. This was not the case at all and just a lack of confidence on my part. That's how I knew I would benefit greatly from participating as often as they would invite me to join the group.

Over the years I did increase my level of confidence, but I did not have the perseverance and consistency necessary to make a lasting and impactful change in my life. Instead, I would return home after each of these conferences fired up and ready to make things happen and then allow my daily life and routine to get the better of me. Within a week I had usually forgotten most of what I had learned and experienced. Looking back, if I had stayed connected with one or two of the other teachers from the conference that would have made the difference. Just having a like-minded individual to discuss things with is sometimes all it takes to help you move forward.

There are quite a few components of leadership we will discuss in this chapter. They include, but are not limited to:

- Communication Skills
- Commitment
- Courage
- Team building
- Goal setting
- Ethics/Character
- Diversity/Tolerance
- Attitude
- Vision/Mission
- Passion/Inspiration
- Public Speaking
- Execution

Leaders Both Lead and Allow Themselves to Be Led

Let's begin with a more general discussion of what a leader is and why this is such as important part of rethinking your work ethic.

A leader leads. We all possess this ability and exhibit this power when we are under duress, such as when there is an emergency situation. This is a physiological phenomenon that we have all heard about, yet few of us realize we can have almost full control over when this occurs in our own mind and body. For now, suffice it to say that once you make the conscious decision to be a leader the skills will strengthen and grow for you.

At times we must be led. Even though I continue to describe myself as an excellent helper, I now have no issue stepping up into a leadership position and role whenever the need arises or I am called upon to do so by others or due to a set of circumstances. The world is a much more effective environment when leaders think through situations, make decisions, take action, and delegate responsibility to others in a well thought out, orderly manner.

Think back to a time in your life where you were called upon to lead. Now think back to a time when you were called upon to assist a leader. Can you see the need for both scenarios in your life?

I believe I will spend the remainder of my life working on both of these areas, and to do so most effectively requires an ongoing study and practice of the key components of leadership I bulleted at the beginning of this chapter. Let's explore each of these more closely now.

Components of Leadership

Communication is at the root of most interpersonal problems that arise, and improving your skills in this area is not only worthwhile, but mandatory if you are to achieve optimal results. So, how do we achieve this goal? By throwing ourselves into the mix as often as possible

Over the years I have increased my willingness to butt into situations and attempt to be of assistance to others. Most recently I was at the post office when a customer had a complete meltdown. I proceeded slowly and with caution but was able to diffuse the situation using my words, facial expressions, and body language. I can remember thinking at the time that the "old me" would not have made contact with this person and instead would have slipped out the door to leave others to get involved.

Now I am not saying that I am always as successful with my communications, but I will tell you that the only way to improve your skills in this area is by ongoing and consistent practice, reviewing the outcome, and then through additional, thoughtful practice.

Commitment is what you have when you feel an obligation and a duty to another person or to a cause. I take this to the extreme and consider it to be tantamount to the covenant we make with God. Yes, it's the ultimate agreement you make with your higher power and applies to life and business in general as well. Use the word commitment with others to show them you are serious about your goals and intentions with them and observe the difference this can make in your life.

Courage comes into play on a daily basis if you stop to think about it. Every day that I work for myself and make things happen with my writing, creation, and development requires me to be courageous. Taking the easy way, such as by taking and staying with a job that will provide you with a regular paycheck but will never give you the life you want and deserve shows a lack of courage on your part. Instead, experience the feeling you'll have when you are willing to be courageous and step into your power and full potential. This may seem risky at the time. Push through your fear and objections and step into the life you were intended to live.

Team building is something I was not familiar with until I attended the camps I described earlier in this book. Once I was a part of those experiences I understood just how beneficial it would have been to participate in team building activities while I was working in real estate or as a classroom teacher.

I now include these types of activities within my mentor programs and at all of my live events, workshops, and retreats and the feedback and results have been incredible over time. There is something about working together with others to push past and through obstacles that makes you glad to be alive. This is also related to my earlier discussion of being a part of a tribe.

Goal setting and achieving is something that is a part of my daily ritual, in that each morning I review my goals for the day before starting my work or other activities. I also review weekly, monthly, quarterly, and annually to see if I'm on track or need to course correct at that time. Thinking of myself as someone who creates value in one way or another for others helps me to further refine my goals so that my time and talents are best utilized. I will share with you that your goals must be written down and reviewed regularly in order to come to fruition in the way you are intending.

Ethics and character come into play almost daily in our lives. Character is defined as the moral qualities distinctive to an individual and ethics are the moral principles that govern and guide our behavior. More than just knowing something is right or wrong, your character and ethics will help determine your ability to engage in fair play that is beneficial to everyone involved. A leader quickly alienates others if they are perceived as being unfair, judgmental, or dishonest in their decisions and interactions with others.

Acceptance of diversity and tolerance of others must be learned in many cases. I believe it was when the Museum of Tolerance opened its doors in Los Angeles in 1993 that I first became aware of how intolerable many of us are when it comes to accepting and empathizing with people throughout the world who are distinctly different from ourselves. I was well into adulthood at that time and remember feeling ashamed of myself for some of the thoughts and beliefs I had harbored over the years in regards to people whose lives I was not familiar with or regularly exposed to. On that day I made the conscious decision to remind myself to have an open mind and attitude when it came to people from all walks of life and from locations and cultures I had not studied, visited, or ever thought about during my lifetime. This has led to some friendships that have broadened my outlook on the world and enriched my life experience.

Striving for and maintaining a positive attitude changes how you view the world around you and the people who inhabit it. Even though life can sometimes serve you some harsh realities, staying positive about the outcome and what you can bring about in the future will certainly make a difference in everything you do.

Vision and Mission are two sides of the same coin. I define my vision as being the overall life goals I strive to accomplish throughout my lifetime. Your personal vision will encompass your core values, your passions, what you believe to be your purpose, and how you envision your life. When writing this down, be specific and clear so that others will understand your meaning and intention. Your vision should embody your view of the future without being too generic. Your vision is also likely to change over time.

My mission is related to the specific areas of my life I am involved with at any given time and should be written down as a Mission Statement. Here is the Mission Statement of Denise Morrison, CEO of the Campbell Soup Company:

"To serve as a leader, live a balanced life, and apply ethical principles to make a significant difference in the world."

Passion and inspiration go hand in hand and are perhaps the most controversial of all the components of leadership. As an employee you have little or no control over what happens with your work. Like my experiences as a classroom teacher, big changes meant that my passion dwindled and my inspiration was at an all time low. I would say that one of my primary reasons for starting my own business was to bring back my passion for life and to receive inspiration from the people and projects I could choose to be involved with every day. True leaders are passionate about their lives and work and can more easily inspire others to reach or exceed their highest potential.

Public speaking is a requirement for leadership in that you must have a way to get your message out to others besides simply writing books and other materials. Your voice identifies you as someone who can not only communicate well but also speak on the topics you are known for. Earlier I wrote about my own experiences with becoming a public speaker. My recommendation is to take every opportunity to speak in front of others so that you become more comfortable sharing your thoughts and idea in this way.

Execution is the final component of leadership. We can jump up and down until we are blue in face, but unless we execute it is of little value. Taking action is a huge step in this process, but executing involves carrying out your plan and seeing through to the end. Leaders never quit or give up. Begin by observing your own behavior to see if you are already someone who follows through with what you say and plan to accomplish. This crucial last step makes all of the difference.

You now have the tools to move to the next level as a leader. People are waiting for you, so do not let them down. As you continue to rethink your work ethic, step into a position of power as a leader in your life and business.

Part V Action Steps

Motivation is what gets you started.
Habit is what keeps you going.
~ Jim Rohn

Now let's take a closer look at the process, thinking of yourself as a specialist, becoming a local celebrity, and being perceived as the leader and how each of these applies to where you are right now in your life and business.

Within the pages of these chapters included in this final section are some concepts that can, if approached and implemented properly, help you to become a successful entrepreneur with a lucrative business model.

What does your process involve when it goes from initial thought, idea, and inception through the project stages of development and on to the final product? Write down the steps you take, making note of those that are vague and those that are more completely fleshed out in your business.

Are you more of a specialist or a generalist? Did one area begin for you because you pursued it, or were you thrust into that position by circumstance? What are your goals in this area for the future?

Have you ever thought of yourself as a celebrity in your field or within a geographic region? How can this concept assist you in furthering your goals? What's the next step?

Are you perceived as a leader? Which of the components I discussed are you drawn to more naturally, and which ones do you now know you need more work in developing? Write down the qualities you believe that you already possess and why you feel this way. Also make a list of the qualities you know you need more work in, along with some ideas and a plan to make these become a part of your nature and disposition.

Summary

I skate to where the puck is going to be,
not to where it has been.
~ Wayne Gretsky

We have now come full circle within the pages of this book while exploring what it will mean to you to rethink your work ethic, embrace the struggle, and exceed your own potential. Beginning with a discussion of work ethic in general we have now arrived at the door to your future through the steps and actions I have prescribed and presented here.

While researching this topic I spoke to more than a hundred friends, acquaintances, small business owners, and other people I know and respect from all walks of life. This resulted in conversations that were at times heated, and we tended to vehemently disagree on more points than we agreed upon each time we engaged in discussions along these lines. But one thing was clear to me from the very beginning, and that is the fact that people all over the world understand that work ethic is something to be studied, discussed, incorporated into the fabric of your being, and made a part of your daily life.

In the first section of this book we looked at the very core of what is meant by the phrase work ethic, based on historical, religious, economic, and political understanding and belief system over the recent centuries. Then I described what I mean by "the struggle" and why embracing the very thing you struggle with is the first and most crucial step in your journey to succeed in life and in business.

A discussion of why this is so important followed, with emphasis on doing the things we think we cannot do, along with Case Studies of some people who live with a strong work ethic every single day and how you can begin to incorporate some of these traits, habits, and strategies into your own life.

Part Three introduced the "what if?" of rethinking the work ethic and went into more detail around the concepts of why your life will be different once you begin to put some of these ideas into motion. We also explored the importance and value of seeing your life and your business in a different light once you make the transition from taking a "transactional" perspective to pursuing a "relational" one in everything you do and undertake.

In the fourth section we dug in our heels to learn how exactly to bring everything you wish to achieve together into a workable format. I shared how you can develop a stronger work ethic, the steps you must take, and a day in the life of someone who lives this as a Mission and Vision.

Finally, we moved forward in the fifth section by taking a closer look at what's next when you embrace the struggle and exceed your own potential. I discussed your potential with the process as a specialist, a local celebrity, and a leader among your peers and colleagues.

The ball is now in your court to make this happen for yourself. If you are to bring to fruition the concepts, ideas, and strategies we have only briefly touched upon together here, then you must take a lead to move from where you are today to closer to where you would like to be.

Years ago they conducted a study with young children five and six years of age. Each child met with one psychologist in a small room. They were each offered one chocolate covered marshmallow right then, and told that if they waited for five minutes they could have two instead. They set up a simple countdown timer so that the child could sit down and wait for five minutes, ring a bell, and have the two chocolate marshmallows brought in to them immediately.

They followed the children in this study on through age twenty-two to see what they were like and how their lives were coming along. It's not surprising that the children who were willing to be patient and wait out the five minutes in order to have twice the reward were the ones who had experienced far more successes and accomplishments in their lives so far.

I would have been one of the children who preferred to have my chocolate marshmallow now instead of waiting for two later on. Impatience and lack of trust and confidence were the predominant forces at work in my life. Since implementing the strategies and techniques I'm writing about here I have become someone will infinite patience and understanding of life's situations. These days I would gladly wait so much longer than five minutes to receive twice as much of something I truly wanted, knowing that patience is a virtue and that the journey is such a valuable part of our life experience.

Imagine yourself living in a different way almost immediately after implementing what you have learned. What will it be like to exceed your own potential with every action you undertake?

Conclusion

*Nothing builds self-esteem and self-confidence
like accomplishment.*
~ Thomas Carlyle

Within the pages of these seventeen chapters I have covered a variety ideas and concepts, some of which may have already been familiar to you and others that may have been mostly unfamiliar, unchartered territory in your realm of consciousness up until now. The next steps are entirely up to you. The actions, or inactions you choose to implement in your life and business in the coming days and weeks will determine the course of the remainder of your life. Choose wisely.

I would advise you to reread this book in whole or in part as you approach this bold new world. If you have been inspired or motivated or even slightly intrigued by what I have shared with you, then make a serious effort to explore these concepts as a course of study. My recommendation is that you continue writing in your notebook or journal, either by hand or in an online document to get the most possible out of this. It's your journey and you will dictate the path you take and the outcome.

Years ago some of the people who read one of my earlier books contacted me to let me know they had formed an online study group to go through my book and implement what I was teaching. They asked me if I would join them on a webinar to discuss their process if they kept it up for a period of time. I agreed and saw how beneficial it was for people to work together in this way. If you make the decision to form such a group, know that you have my full support along the way.

Life and business are team efforts, and it will behoove you to surround yourself with the people who you want on your team. It is incumbent upon all of us to work hard, bring forth our greatest gifts and talents to share with others, and to live each day knowing we can exceed our own potential.

About the Author

Wouldn't take nothing for my journey now.
~ Maya Angelou

Connie Ragen Green is an online marketing strategist, bestselling author, international speaker, and mentor to people on six continents. She is a former classroom teacher and real estate broker and appraiser who left it all behind to start an online business during 2006.

After struggling during her first year, Connie finally embraced the struggles of writing and technology, leveled up her work ethic, and continues to exceed her own potential in her life and business.

Making her home in two cities, Santa Barbara, California at the beach and Santa Clarita, California in the desert, Connie is active with a number of charities, non-profits, and service organizations. These include Rotary, an international service organization, Zonta, a women's business organization, the Benevolent and Protective Order of Elk, the Boys and Girls Clubs of America, and SEE International.

Becoming an online entrepreneur changed Connie's life forever. Once she became versed in online marketing and observed first-hand how powerful the effect was for people all over the world, she began writing on a variety of topics, creating information products, speaking at live events and workshops, and mentoring people on how to build a successful and lucrative business they can run from home or from anywhere in the world.

Find out more by visiting http://ConnieRagenGreen.com to connect with Connie and to begin your own journey of online entrepreneurship.

www.ingramcontent.com/pod-product-compliance
Lightning Source LLC
Chambersburg PA
CBHW060037210326
41520CB00009B/1168